Barbara Kimenye

Taxi!

J·A·W·S

Illustrated by
Paul Collicutt

Series editor: Rod Nesbitt

HEINEMANN

Heinemann Educational
a division of Heinemann Publishers (Oxford) Ltd
Halley Court, Jordan Hill, Oxford OX2 8EJ

Heinemann Educational Boleswa
PO Box 10103, Village Post Office, Gaborone, Botswana
Heinemann Educational Books (Nigeria) Ltd
PMB 5205, Ibadan

FLORENCE PRAGUE PARIS MADRID
ATHENS JOHANNESBURG MELBOURNE
AUCKLAND PORTSMOUTH (NH) CHICAGO
SINGAPORE TOKYO SAO PAULO

British Library Cataloguing in Publication Data
A catalogue record for this book is available from the British Library

ISBN 0 435 89363 7

Glossary
African words are listed alphabetically on page 110

Printed and bound in Great Britain by
Cox & Wyman Ltd, Reading, Berkshire

93 94 95 96 10 9 8 7 6 5 4 3 2 1

Chapter One

When Paulo felt, rather than heard, the sickening crunch of bone and flesh under the wheels, he pressed hard on the accelerator, ignoring the shouts of alarm from the people who rushed, as if from nowhere, to what was now lying in the road. At the same time, the sound of broken glass told him that at least one of his headlamps was badly damaged.

But he dared not stop the car. If that angry crowd caught him, he knew only too well what to expect. They would wreck the vehicle and might beat him to death. It would not matter that the accident had not been his fault.

True, he had been travelling at nearly 100 kph on a busy road, but the victim had obviously been dead drunk. The man had swayed at the side of the road, and then fallen straight into the path of Paulo's oncoming car.

Drunkards were always a menace on a Saturday night. Lucky for Paulo that he was not carrying a passenger at the time. A passenger would have proved a dangerous complication.

As it was, he would have to drive over to the Kisenyi and find a garage with mechanics who knew how to keep their mouths shut, before the police started to ask questions.

He only hoped that nobody had remembered the

car's number, not that it was likely at the speed he had been travelling on that stretch of badly lit road. Nevertheless, it would be wise to have new plates made. Changing the actual registration letters and numerals was unnecessary. New plates with the letters parallel with the numbers, instead of above them, was all that was needed. It was surprising what a difference the change made to anybody on the look-out for letters and numbers in the original order.

Anybody who had supplied details of the registration number to the police was sure to have second thoughts when they saw the new plates. And it was perfectly legal.

While thinking about this, Paulo left the main Masaka Road and took one of the *murram* tracks which, although it snaked all over Rubaga and Mmengo, lessened the risk of his meeting a police patrol car. Soon he was in the comparative safety of the Kisenyi.

The Kisenyi never slept. This sprawling collection of mud and wattle houses, tiny kiosks operating as general shops, and 'hotelis', was as alive at midnight as it was at midday. There was no street lighting. All the light needed came from open fires or charcoal stoves on which people cooked their food, as well as the hot, hissing pressure lamps lighting the open-fronted kiosks and butchers' stalls.

Late as it was, a man was driving a herd of goats along the narrowest of alleys. Paulo was forced to stop his car as he shouted at the goat-herd and his bleating charges. Other people were shouting too because the animals had wedged themselves in a solid mass, not wanting to squeeze between the houses and the car. They preferred to step daintily through open doorways in which women lounged and laughed. When these housewives did at last manage to drive the goats away, angry words were exchanged over the goats' droppings.

Paulo soon found the garage he was looking for. The man who owned it was sitting on the steps of his ramshackle house, listening to a transistor radio. Even in the night gloom it was possible to see that his compound was littered with the shapeless bits of dismantled vehicles. The garage itself was a canopy of corrugated iron held up on wooden poles. The garage owner did not say much when Paulo asked if he could fit a new headlamp rightaway. He brought an electric torch to examine the extent of the damage, crouching down to see more clearly.

'Where did this blood come from?' he asked, running a finger over a dried red splash in a deep dent on the front bumper.

'I hit a dog,' Paulo replied. Without a word, the garage owner ambled away for a cloth and water, and removed the stain.

He was longer in finding a headlamp rim and glass to fit Paulo's particular model of car. But as soon as he started on the replacement job, he hardly opened his mouth except to ask Paulo to pass the pliers or a screwdriver. He accepted the payment he had asked for with a brief nod, and it was arranged that Paulo would return next day to have the dent beaten out of the bumper.

He brought an electric torch to examine the extent of
the damage.

As Paulo climbed into the driving seat he said, 'By the way, can you fix me up with a couple of new number plates? These on the car are hopeless. Look how the enamel is peeling.'

The garage owner wandered around the car to stare at both registration plates.

'I could touch these up for you, if you like,' he said. Paulo shook his head.

'No, thanks. I'd rather have new ones. I fancy those long white plates with black letters.'

The garage owner picked his nose.

'They don't go well on cars as small as this,' he argued.

'I'd like to try them,' Paulo persisted. 'Anyway, do you think you can do it?'

'You can easily buy what you want in Kampala,' the garage owner said.

'I know, but I thought perhaps they would be cheaper from you,' Paulo said, smiling at the same time.

The garage owner turned to walk back to his original position outside his house.

'I'll see what I can find before you come back tomorrow,' he grunted.

Paulo switched on the engine and the lights, and glanced at the dashboard. The clock said that the time was past one o'clock in the morning. He would just be in time to pick up people leaving the nightclubs, and he knew he would have to keep busy if he was to make up the money paid to the garage owner. With a wave to the garage owner, now nursing the transistor radio which was playing loud music from Zaire, Paulo swung the car round to face the gap in the sagging fence which was the only entry and exit to the compound.

As he did so, he was immediately blinded by the approach of powerful headlamps. He braked wildly, and broke out in a cold sweat as shouts and police whistles sounded on every side.

Chapter Two

Before Paulo had time to think, and with the strong headlights still blazing directly into his eyes, rough hands dragged him from the car and propelled him towards the garage owner's house.

Policemen swarmed everywhere, directing the beam of their torches over the piles of rusting junk and old vehicles littering the compound.

In front of the house, the garage owner continued to nurse his transistor radio, but he was held by two constables and he was being questioned by a police inspector. The man's family, a tearful middle-aged woman in a crumpled *suka*, and a group of frightened children, clustered in the doorway, too terrified to move.

Beyond the compound, the Kisenyi had suddenly quietened. The mere sight of the police was enough to send the residents scurrying inside their houses. Cooking was left to burn, and doors securely closed and bolted. The Kisenyi, with its overcrowded hovels housing what prosperous Ugandans regarded as thieves and murderers, attracted criminals from all over East Africa. Living there, a person never knew when a friend or neighbour might have his house raided, and he himself pulled in for questioning by the police as an accomplice.

As Paulo was marched towards the house, a police officer emerged carrying a pile of log books, driving licences and other documents. A constable took them from him and carried them to one of the patrol cars.

'And who is this?' the officer asked, hands on hips, inspecting Paulo.

'He's a taxi-driver,' the garage owner replied.

'What's he doing here at this time of night?' the officer wanted to know.

Paulo held his breath until the garage owner said, 'He was enquiring after somebody I've never heard of.'

'Who were you looking for?' This time the officer spoke directly to Paulo, who gulped before answering, 'Oh, it was somebody called … er … called Abu Ssentongo. He owes me some money.'

The officer stared hard at him.

'What made you think he would be here?'

Paulo tried to keep the fear out of his voice.

'He told me that he stayed here.'

The inspector gave a nasty chuckle.

'Well, it looks as though you've been fooled,' he laughed. 'It isn't often that somebody gets the better of a taxi-driver.'

Paulo was beginning to relax, when the police officer suddenly shouted at him, 'What's your name? And how long have you known him?' With a jerk of his thumb, he indicated the garage owner.

'He doesn't know me,' the garage owner protested. 'He only —'

'Let him answer for himself,' the officer said.

'I don't know him. I came here to find the man who owes me money. That's all,' Paulo muttered, avoiding the garage owner's eyes.

'And who is this?' the officer asked.

The police officer turned his attention to the garage owner, warning the man that he would be wise to tell where the stolen cars came from and give them any other motor vehicle documents he had.

The garage owner remained stubbornly silent. He didn't say a word, even when the police started to load most of the old vehicles in his compound on to a police lorry. Then they pushed him into the back of a police car and drove away.

Paulo felt sick when a constable grabbed him by the arm and shouted, 'What about this one, sir?'

He almost fainted with relief when the officer called back, 'Oh, he can go.'

Two constables walked with him to his car, as if they had nothing better to do, and he prayed that they would not notice the trembling of his limbs or the sweat breaking out on his brow.

He now realised that the police raid had nothing to do with him. Somebody must have told the police that the garage owner was selling stolen vehicle documents, as well as receiving stolen cars and breaking them down for spare parts. Still, after what had happened earlier on the Masaka Road, Paulo wanted to put as much distance as possible between himself and the nearest policeman.

Without a word, he climbed into his car and started the engine. The two constables came closer as he switched on the lights.

'Look at that!' exclaimed one of them. 'You've had a nasty knock. Look at this front bumper.'

Somehow, Paulo gritted his teeth and put the car in

gear. He skidded out of the garage owner's compound before the constables had time to examine the bumper, and headed for the Bongo Club on the other side of Mmengo.

◇

There was such a crush of people at both bars that it was difficult to get a drink, and the air was thick with cigarette smoke and the smell of beer.

Paulo took one look at the mass of people inside, and decided to sit on the veranda with some other taxi-drivers. They were all drinking soft drinks, since very few of them ever touched anything stronger.

'Where have you been all night?' a young driver called Musa asked Paulo. 'You missed some good business earlier on. There was a big wedding party over at Port Bell.'

Paulo lit a cigarette and replied, 'Oh, I had a bit of engine trouble, so I went to the Kisenyi to get it fixed. I was held up there because the police decided to raid the man just as I was leaving.'

'No!' Musa looked startled.

'What's that? A police raid?' another man asked. 'Are you talking about Bosa – the fat man?'

The taxi-drivers, six of them, drew closer to Paulo and made him tell the full story, or as much of it as he wanted to tell them.

When he finished, an elderly driver, Peter Waswa, said, 'I'm glad you told us. I was going to call on Bosa tomorrow and see if he had any second-hand tyres.'

'If, as Paulo says, he can't account for the stuff the police found at his place, I suppose it will mean at least seven years inside,' Musa remarked. 'Why on earth didn't he hide everything?'

'It's his family I feel sorry for,' Peter said.

'Yes,' Paulo nodded. 'The wife and children were howling their heads off when the police took him away. Still, he must have made plenty of money.'

'I doubt if he had enough to keep a family going for any length of time,' grunted Peter. 'I'd better call and see if they need any help sometime. After all, that man has always dealt fairly with us.'

The other taxi-drivers backed him up.

'Yes, Peter,' one said, 'let us know what we can do to help. We can always take up a collection among ourselves and any other drivers who feel like helping the Bosa family.'

The conversation changed when somebody told Peter of a place on Hoima Road where car tyres were available.

'But,' the man warned, 'there's no point in going until after ten o'clock at night. The brothers dealing in tyres are supposed to be cobblers.'

The drivers continued to talk about ways and means of getting spare parts more cheaply than on the open market. Paulo scarcely listened. He was thinking of the dent in his front bumper, and the need to find a fresh set of registration plates. It might be better to take the car over to Jinja, and have it fixed. The police might be carrying out a series of raids on suspect garages in Kampala, and it was stupid to take any chances. Yes,

Paulo thought, I'll drive to Jinja first thing in the morning, then I'll be all right.

One by one the other taxi-drivers left to take people wherever they wanted to go, until only old Peter and Paulo remained.

'You are very quiet tonight,' Peter observed. 'What's the matter? Are you getting tired of this life?'

'Tired? What do you mean?' Paulo moved uneasily in his chair, and lit another cigarette to avoid looking directly at Peter.

'You know what I mean,' Peter went on. 'We taxi-drivers can make good money, but for youngsters like you – how old are you now, Paulo? Twenty-two? Twenty-three? Well, for youngsters like you, there's very little fun. Driving other folk all over the place to enjoy themselves while you spend nearly every waking hour sitting in a car.

'You must often wish you were one of the passengers, instead of the driver. And in this job, what are your chances of finding a nice girl and settling down?'

Paulo laughed. 'It doesn't take me long to find a woman when I want one.'

Peter slowly shook his head.

'I'm sure you can. But what really sensible girl wants a man who is out most of the night, and not always in for meals during the day?'

'Well, you managed it!' Paulo replied. 'Your Susanna never complains about the amount of time you spend on the road.'

It was Peter's turn to laugh. 'Susanna! She's different. She comes from a family of taxi-drivers, and she drives as well as I do! Did you know that Susanna and I were introduced by her brother – the one who now runs his own car-hire firm in Nairobi?'

Just then a man and a girl approached them, asking to be driven to Makerere.

'You take them,' Peter told Paulo. 'I'm beginning to feel my age. I think I'll go straight home.'

'Goodnight!' Paulo called, as he led the couple to his car. The talk with Peter had made him feel better. Things seemed much more normal, and it was time, Paulo told himself, to put the accident out of his thoughts. Accidents happened every day on Ugandan roads. Surely one more would not make much difference.

When the couple paid him off at Makerere, four other people climbed into his taxi and asked to be driven to a popular bar in the city. Soon, Paulo was caught up in the usual end-of-month weekend excitement. As fast as one load of passengers left his car, another jumped in. Apart from a brief stop at a petrol station, he was busy driving for the next two hours.

After dropping three noisy young men back at the Bongo Club, Paulo decided to go home and have a rest. After all, he wanted to be on his way to Jinja early in the morning, before there was much traffic on the road.

There was still a group of taxis parked at one end of the carpark, but their drivers were talking quietly among themselves outside the entrance to the club.

'Paulo!' one of them shouted, as Paulo was about to drive off. 'Wait a minute, Paulo!'

Paulo idled the engine while Musa ran to him and peered anxiously into the car.

'Have you heard?' Musa asked.

Paulo frowned. 'Heard what?'

'One of Peter's sons was knocked down on the Masaka Road, earlier tonight – and the boy died in Mulago Hospital about an hour ago!'

Chapter Three

Paulo hardly saw the road as he drove home. Peter's son! He had killed Peter's son. Until Musa told him of the boy's death, he had never thought of the body crushed beneath his wheels as a person with a name and a family. Paulo's main concern had been to make sure no one suspected him. It had certainly not crossed his mind that the accident victim might be someone he knew.

Tomorrow, or rather today, since it was already after five o'clock, promised to be an agonising day. He would have to attend the funeral to show respect for Peter, who was the leader of their particular group of taxi-drivers. Peter had taught many of them to drive, as well as helping them raise money to buy their first vehicles. Also, Peter could be counted on to sort out problems with the police who sometimes turned nasty over threadbare tyres or what they claimed to be defective brakes.

As for his wife, Susanna, she was always ready to lend money to a driver booked for a long-distance job which called for a larger than usual purchase of petrol before he was paid. Altogether, she was a wonderful, understanding woman. Paulo dreaded having to look her in the face, knowing that he was responsible for her grief.

And he had no doubt that he was responsible. Although accidents were frequent on that particular stretch of road, it was unlikely that two serious accidents would have occurred at roughly the same time.

He was sick with guilt and fear when he reached the house in Kibuye where he rented a room. Sleep was out of the question. He stretched out on his narrow bed, and smoked one cigarette after another.

Shortly after eight o'clock that same morning, he was up and dressed in his shabbiest clothes, as a sign of mourning. After a quick cup of tea, he set off for the funeral.

Traditionally, he would be expected to sit with the grieving family until the burial took place in the afternoon. The drive out to Peter's home at Natete was a nightmare. The nearer Paulo drew, the more he wished for a head-on collision with a heavy vehicle which would put him out of his misery. As he passed the spot where the accident had occurred, his heart thudded uncomfortably. Again, he wondered whether some sharp-sighted witness had noticed the car's registration number, and the angry stare of a woman waiting to cross the road brought him out in a sweat.

Outside Peter's house, Paulo parked at the end of a long line of cars, and hoped his dented bumper would go unnoticed. Normally it would, because very few taxis were without minor damage. But at a time like this, he was sure that any recent scratch or dent would arouse suspicion.

Inside the house, Susanna, worn out through weeping and dressed in a faded *kikoyi* and an old blouse, was wailing with other women in the largest room where the body was laid out on a mattress.

Peter, red-eyed and seemingly grown older in the past few hours, clasped Paulo's hand and led him through to the back veranda where the men of his family and clan, as well as a large gathering of taxi-drivers, were sitting in silence. Greetings were exchanged in quiet voices.

It was late in the afternoon when the grave-diggers finished their work in the back *shamba*, and the coffin was delivered. A minister from Namirembe Cathedral arrived to read the funeral service. Throughout the long hours before and during the burial, Paulo wanted more than anything else to throw himself at Susanna's and Peter's feet, and confess his part in their son's death. He had forced himself to view the body, and the sight of the eighteen-year-old boy, Charles, youngest of Susanna's and Peter's five children, lying dead, made him tremble.

It was useless to recall that Charles had been a constant source of trouble to the family, with his heavy drinking and the fact that he could not keep a job for more than a week. Because of his drinking, Charles, unlike the rest of Peter's family, had never been allowed to drive a car. Nothing altered the fact, however, that Charles held a special place in the affections of his parents, and was generally popular with everybody who knew him.

The funeral was over by early evening. The tears and the wailing had done their work. The mourners were exhausted. As people began leaving, Peter explained to the small group remaining on the veranda that he held no grudge against whoever had knocked down his son.

'Charles was probably drunk,' he said. 'Susanna says she could smell *waragi* on his clothes. But …' here Peter raised his head and looked directly at the men around him, 'what I cannot forgive is the driver refusing to stop, or, as far as I know, report the accident to the police.'

Over the murmurs of agreement, he added, 'You young drivers must always remember what I keep telling you about such accidents. Stop immediately, even if you are sure the accident is not your fault. Pick up the person concerned, and take him to the nearest hospital or police station – no matter how slight his injuries appear to be. If you keep your head and act quickly, an angry mob won't have time to get at you!'

A driver called Musoke asked how far the police were in tracing the accident vehicle.

Peter sadly shook his head. 'What can they do? It was too dark for anybody to see anything clearly. I believe that one woman living near the scene of the accident claims that the car involved was very like a taxi that often travels past her house, but how can she be sure?'

'You were doing the Masaka Road run this week, Paulo, weren't you?' Musoke spoke easily enough, but Paulo's mouth went dry.

Trying to sound natural, he replied, 'Me and dozens of other taxis. Anyway, I spent most of last night in the Kisenyi, trying to find somebody to fix that knock in the engine.'

'That's right,' Peter said. 'You were there when poor Bosa was raided by the police.'

'You were doing the Masaka Road run this week,
Paulo, weren't you?'

20

It was typical of Peter's thoughtfulness that he immediately asked one of the drivers to check on the Bosa family.

'I can't leave Susanna this evening,' he explained, 'so I'd be grateful if one of you boys would find out what help we can give Mrs Bosa and the children.'

As soon as he could, Paulo excused himself and went home. He had a splitting headache, but felt a little better after a cup of tea.

Musoke, who rented a room in the house next to Paulo's, joined him later in the evening to see if he was doing the usual Sunday nightclub run.

'I don't think I will,' Paulo told him. 'I feel worn out, what with no sleep last night and the funeral today. I think I'll go to bed and have an early start in the morning.'

'Suit yourself,' Musoke said cheerfully. 'With you out of the way, there will be more customers for the rest of us.'

Paulo smiled and walked with him to the outer door.

'By the way,' Musoke suddenly remarked, 'they know the type of car they are looking for. Before I left Peter's place, a policeman came to say they have identified the glass from a headlamp found in the road. It's the same model as yours, which really doesn't mean much, considering how many of the same model there are on the roads.'

Paulo somehow managed to keep control of himself, even when Musoke stared for a moment at the dented front bumper and the repaired headlamp on the car. It was no good wishing that he had parked in the side alley, instead of in front of the house. And was it imagination, or had he really detected a sudden change in Musoke's attitude as he said goodbye?

As soon as he was alone, Paulo returned to his room and sat on the bed, his head in his hands, sweating with terror.

Gradually, he forced himself to calm down, reasoning that Musoke's interest in the damaged bumper and repaired headlamp was nothing to worry about. Musoke didn't know when the damage had occurred. It could have happened weeks ago – which was what Paulo intended to say, should he be asked about it.

Of course, the police would be enquiring about recent headlamp repairs at workshops and garages. But, there again, with Mr Bosa already in their custody, Paulo believed he was safe. He felt, however, that the sooner the bumper was fixed, the better, so he decided to look for another mechanic in the Kisenyi, without wasting any more time.

His first stop in the Kisenyi was Lucia's Hoteli, which was no more than a long mud shack divided into narrow cubicles by hessian curtains. Anybody was welcome to spend a night there for a few shillings.

Lucia had been born and bred in the Kisenyi, and knew all that went on in its crowded streets. Paulo found her sitting on the doorstep of her private quarters, a cigarette dangling from a corner of her mouth, a thin striped kitten on her knee.

She replied to his greeting without removing the cigarette.

'That was a bad business – young Charles killed on the road,' she said. 'I couldn't attend the funeral because that girl you brought here a couple of weeks ago went into labour. The baby was born this afternoon.'

Paulo leaned against the side of his car, and answered her questions about Charles's accident and the funeral arrangements.

Finally Lucia wanted to know the reason for his visit.

'Shouldn't you be on the nightclub run?' she asked. 'Or did you make enough money last night for you to afford to waste time on an old woman like me?'

'You're not so old, Lucia,' he laughed. 'Anyway I came to ask if you know somebody who can do a quick job on my front bumper. Bosa was going to do it – until he was picked up by the police, as you probably know.'

Lucia glanced critically at the dented bumper.

'You must have hit something at a terrific speed,' she commented. 'What was it – a dog?'

'That's right – a dog. A big one too.'

She shrugged. 'It always is, isn't it?'

She thought for a moment and then directed Paulo to a house in a compound surrounded by a mud brick wall, and told him to ask for Sulemani.

Sulemani turned out to be a tough-looking little man about Paulo's own age. He had obviously been interrupted during his evening meal, for he chewed at a leg of roasted chicken while he examined Paulo's car.

'This will take some time,' he announced at last. 'Do you want to leave it here, and collect it tomorrow?'

Paulo explained that he was a taxi-driver.

'Lucia thought you might be able to finish the job tonight,' he said. 'I'm losing money as long as the car is off the road.'

Sulemani threw away the chicken bone and wiped his hands on his dungarees.

'Well, if I take off the bumper, you can still use the car,' he pointed out.

Paulo could not decide which would be more suspicious, a dented bumper or a missing bumper. Sulemani watched him shrewdly while he tried to make up his mind.

'I'll tell you what,' he offered. 'If you don't want to drive around town in a vehicle that advertises that you've been in an accident, how about doing a driving job for some of my friends? We pay well.'

'What sort of job?' Paulo hesitated. He could not say why, but he neither liked nor trusted Sulemani.

'Nothing special,' Sulemani assured him. 'They want to collect some stuff from a place near Mukono, and then call at a house on Tank Hill. You take them, and I'll mend your bumper as well as pay you for your trouble.'

'You mean, use my car without the bumper?'

'No. They have their own car, but their driver didn't turn up this evening.'

Through the open shutters of a window, and in very weak lamplight, Paulo made out the figures of four men eating at a table inside the house. They did not look the sort of people to employ drivers. But who was he to question appearances? He had to admit that Sulemani was offering a fair deal.

He was surprised, however, when he saw the vehicle he was supposed to drive. It was a recent Japanese model, a stationwagon, in perfect condition.

'This is a beautiful car,' he said enviously.

'Don't touch!' Sulemani warned, as Paulo went to stroke the bonnet. 'The spray may not be fully dry.'

Paulo was startled.

'If it goes on the road straight after a respray,' he said, 'it will come back with dust glued to it! And what if we run into some rain?'

Sulemani didn't seem to care.

'Oh, it'll dry soon enough,' he said, 'once you get moving. Now, you wait here. I'll call the others.'

Paulo regretted having accepted the job. He was absolutely certain that the car in front of him was stolen property, probably from neighbouring Kenya, and he did not want to be caught at the wheel. Had it not been for the urgency of getting the bumper on his own car put right, he would have cheerfully walked away from Sulemani and his friends.

Then his feeling of regret changed to real alarm, as a voice came clearly through the open window.

'How do you know we can trust him?'

He heard Sulemani's mocking laugh.

'That taxi-driver has to trust us,' Sulemani said. 'From the state of his car, I'd say he has as much to hide as we have!'

Chapter Four

A few minutes later, Sulemani came out of the house
with the other men. Paulo did not have a clear view of
their faces, but he noted that their clothes were shabby.

Sulemani did not bother with introductions. He
simply told Paulo that the regular driver had taken the
car keys, so the vehicle would have to be started by
means of the loose wires hanging from a hole in the
dashboard where the ignition lock had been removed.
This was enough to confirm Paulo's suspicions that he
was dealing with a stolen car. Wisely, he kept quiet, and
had the engine running by the time the four men had
piled into the car.

Out on the main road, he forgot his passengers in
the pleasure it gave him to be behind the wheel of a
good, well-maintained vehicle. It was the first time he
had driven this latest Japanese model, and he enjoyed
the experience. As they approached Mukono, one of
the men directed him to turn off down a bumpy track.

He was ordered to stop the car but to keep the
engine running, while all four men set out on foot for a
house which was silhouetted among trees some
distance away.

They were gone for about thirty minutes.
Meanwhile, Paulo listened to the car's radio, played at
low volume, and examined the many gadgets with
which the car was fitted. He was playing with the

controls for the airconditioning and the electric windows when the men returned, stumbling under the weight of heavy bundles. Throwing the bundles into the back of the stationwagon, they told him to drive back to Kampala and take them to Tank Hill.

There was more traffic on the main road now, and, because it was something all taxi-drivers did, Paulo flicked his lights and hooted in salute each time he passed a fellow taxi-driver. His passengers didn't like it. They warned him about it and only relaxed when Paulo stopped waving and hooting to greet his colleagues. In any case, he realised, none of them would recognise this smart car as being in the taxi business.

Tank Hill was well populated and he expected to be asked to drive into one of the many groups of small houses usually surrounding a collection of kiosks selling basic foods. He was surprised that people such as the men he was carrying wanted to be driven to an area known to house rich businessmen and diplomats.

When they told him to stop on a quiet track between the huge fenced gardens of two mansions, one of which Paulo knew belonged to a respected lawyer, he almost refused. All that prevented him from stepping from the car, and leaving the four men to carry on with whatever mischief they planned, was the thought of his own car held in Sulemani's compound. As long as Sulemani had the car, Paulo was in no position to argue.

He watched in icy fear as the men crept along the fence and removed one of the iron sheets forming it. It was done so easily that Paulo was sure that the iron sheet must have been loosened some time earlier. Then they disappeared into the garden. There was a cautious rustling as they pushed their way through the thorny bushes which had been planted to keep intruders out.

Paulo tried to avoid looking at the dashboard clock, although he could hear the minutes ticking away. He was tempted to leave the car and hide in the shadows, because this was one Kampala neighbourhood which he was certain would have regular police patrols. To give himself something to do, and because he had a feeling that the track on which he was parked led to a dead end, he carefully turned the car to face the way he had come. His own would never have managed it without plenty of gear-grinding, reversing and advancing, but this Japanese model was a joy to handle. It responded easily to the slightest touch.

He was interrupted in his admiration of the car's performance by the hurried return of his passengers. And he was horrified to see the first two carrying a stereo music centre complete with amplifiers, the third staggering along with a large television set, and the fourth burdened with computing equipment.

Paulo prepared to start the engine and drive off, but as soon as the loot was stacked with the bundles in the back of the stationwagon, the men were again running to scramble through the fence. Their second journey resulted in a carton of imported whisky, and a pile of good quality curtains.

Paulo started off at full speed. It was unnecessary for anybody to tell him twice, after a nightwatchman's whistle sounded, and a dog started frantically barking.

28

He was horrified to see the first two men carrying a
stereo music centre.

He risked overturning the car on corners and bounced through potholes, some of which were quite deep. Even so, the track seemed longer on the way back to the main tarmac road.

The main road was in sight now, and Paulo started to breathe more easily. But when a police patrol car drove out of a side turning, completely blocking his path, he automatically slammed on the brakes and jumped out of the stationwagon without stopping to think.

At the same moment, two policemen leapt from the patrol car and raced forward. Paulo was, for a second, caught in the beam of their electric torches, but he turned and raced wildly into the bushes at the edge of the track, and ran, tripping and stumbling, through waist-high grass. Several times he tripped and fell headlong. His clothes caught on thorns, but he kept going. He kept going until the shouts and other sounds of the chase faded into nothing. By then he had struggled across private property and had almost lost a running battle with an old, yet still fierce, dog.

Gratefully, he flung himself into a ditch, and lay there panting. He was weak from the unfamiliar exercise of the run, as well as from lack of food. He remembered that he had not eaten at all in the past twenty-four hours.

But his biggest worry was his car. He was convinced that the four men who had landed him in this mess must have been caught by the police, and that sooner or later they would lead the police to Sulemani's house. Once there, the police would pay special attention to any vehicle on the premises, including his own.

Although he realised the risk he was taking, Paulo crawled out of the ditch and set off for the Kisenyi. He had to know if there was a chance of removing the car before the arrival of the police.

It was a slow, tiring journey, because he had to move in the dark along rarely used paths. His guide was the distant glow of lighted buildings in the valley. They seemed very far away, and there were moments when Paulo thought he would never reach them.

Then, worn out and desperate, he knocked urgently on Lucia's door. She gasped at the state of his clothes and his terrified face, and drew him inside the house, without a word.

Turning up the wick of an oil lamp, she motioned Paulo to sit on a chair. Lucia herself sat on the untidy bed where the striped kitten dozed quietly among the sheets.

'Would you like a drink while you tell me what happened?' she asked, and Paulo nodded dumbly.

Sipping a glass of neat *waragi*, which relieved the dryness of his mouth and warmed his empty stomach, he told Lucia how he came to be involved with the thieves and explained that he was afraid that he would be traced through his car. Lucia was scornful of Sulemani's part in everything that happened. However, she was confident that Paulo had nothing to worry about.

'Sulemani is crafty and dangerous,' she said, laughing softly. 'Anybody who informs on him is gambling with his life. He makes a very nasty enemy. If those men value their lives, they'll keep quiet.'

Paulo wondered what Sulemani might do to him for running away and abandoning the men and the stationwagon filled with stolen goods.

'He'll do nothing after I've talked to him,' Lucia declared, as she heated a pan of soup on a primus stove. 'Drink this soup as soon as it is ready.'

She tied a *kikoyi* over her crumpled nightdress.

'I'm going to see Sulemani,' she said. 'Believe me, you've nothing to worry about.'

Nothing to worry about! Paulo thought Lucia would soon change her mind about that, if she knew why he needed to have the car bumper repaired.

The soup was thick and greasy. He ate to fill his grumbling stomach, even though it made him feel slightly sick. Afterwards, he stretched out on Lucia's bed and immediately fell asleep, the striped kitten purring softly at his side. He was awakened an hour later by Lucia shaking his shoulder.

'Come on. Your car is waiting for you outside,' she said.

Briefly she explained that the police had not been near Sulemani, who was furious to learn of the wrecking of the night's plan. For his own protection, in case any or all of his four friends should be persuaded to talk, he had personally removed Paulo's car from his premises, and driven it to Lucia's door.

'Lucia, I don't know how to thank you!' Paulo exclaimed.

'You can thank me by being a good boy and keeping out of trouble,' she said, opening the door for him to leave.

Standing outside her house, Paulo noticed with relief that Sulemani had kept his promise and repaired the bumper. For the moment, his troubles seemed to be over. He drove home through the now quiet streets, and fell asleep as soon as his head touched the pillow.

◇

Next morning Paulo drove straight to the market, the regular meeting place for Peter's group of taxi-drivers. Most of the drivers were already drinking tea in Janti's Cafe, which they had adopted as their headquarters.

Being Monday, there was not much business. Kampala housewives had done their heaviest shopping on the previous Saturday, and while the market appeared to be bustling, most of the shoppers were house servants who were expected to carry home their purchases on foot or by bus.

Paulo strolled into Janti's. At a table in the centre, Musa was finishing a story which already had his companions roaring with laughter.

'So I said to her,' Musa continued, as Paulo approached, 'I said, Madam, I won't charge you for the baby, or the stacks of *matoke* – but that goat isn't travelling free!'

Paulo joined in the laughter, sat down and ordered a cup of coffee. He listened calmly as the conversation turned from peculiar passengers to football, and added his opinion to those given on the national team's chances against the visiting Zimbabweans.

His first uncomfortable moment came when he

picked up a newspaper lying on the table. He could not resist feverishly searching for some mention of the Tank Hill house robbery, or of some house which had been robbed near Mukono, for he now suspected that the first house visited by the four men had also been robbed.

Of course, there was nothing about either in the newspaper. Both incidents had occurred after the paper had gone to press.

'What are you looking so worried about?' Paulo jumped as Musoke took a seat opposite him and asked the question.

'No, I'm not worried,' Paulo tried to laugh. 'I was reading the crime reports. There isn't much else in the papers, these days.'

Musoke ordered tea for himself, and grumbled, 'You're right. If the police spent less time chasing us for so-called traffic offences, they would catch more crooks.'

Paulo flashed him a look of mock surprise.

'Oh ho! So you have been caught again, have you? What was it this time? Speeding?'

'No. Overloading,' Musoke replied. 'I was taking some of Peter's relatives back to Bombo. They spent the night with Peter and Susanna after the funeral. I had hardly hit the road before a police cop stopped me and made six passengers get out.'

'How many were you carrying?' Paulo asked suspiciously.

Musoke gave Paulo an innocent look.

'Only eleven!' he replied. 'And you know that a car

like mine can squeeze in as many as thirteen!'

For the next few minutes, he and Paulo chatted about the number of passengers which various makes of car could hold. But beneath Paulo's joking and easy manner was a growing fear that Musoke would ask about the dented bumper and the repaired headlamp.

Soon, Paulo's nerves were stretched to breaking point. Without knowing why he did it, he suddenly blurted out, 'By the way, I had that damaged bumper repaired.'

The moment the words were out of his mouth, he knew they were a mistake. There was a pause. Musoke's eyes flickered, then became blank.

'I never knew that there was anything wrong with it,' he said evenly.

He excused himself on the pretence of asking another driver about the man's sick wife.

Paulo knew that he had made a fool of himself by trying to find out whether or not Musoke had seen something suspicious in the damage to his car. Now he had given Musoke good reason to believe that all was not as it should be. He comforted himself with the thought of the unwritten rule among taxi-drivers. This said simply that no questions were asked about car damage, unless it was really serious, and under no circumstances was information about one of their number to be passed on to the police.

He ran his eyes over the sports page of the newspaper in an effort to calm his anxiety. He was deep in a feature article concerning traditional wrestling, when he was aware of the abrupt halt to all the talk going on around him.

Raising his head to see what was causing this uncomfortable silence, Paulo had difficulty preventing a howl escaping his lips. In the doorway of the cafe stood two police constables – and they looked as though they meant business.

Chapter Five

The blood pounded so noisily in Paulo's ears that he was convinced everybody else in the cafe must be able to hear it. He nearly choked on the unpleasant lump in his throat, and he felt himself glued to his seat. Beads of sweat broke out on his forehead and upper lip.

One of the policemen glanced at his notebook.

'Who are the drivers of USN95, UTR178 and UTO74 parked in the road outside?' he asked in a loud voice.

There was a slight murmur, and three drivers got up, fumbling in pockets for their driving licences. The policemen examined the licences, then asked the drivers to accompany them to where the cars were parked.

'What can they be looking for?' somebody muttered anxiously. 'I've never known the police trouble us here in Janti's.'

Paulo held his breath. Each of the drivers taken by the police drove cars very similar to his own.

'Oh, didn't you know?' another driver replied. 'They're jumping on anybody with an out-of-date road licence. Surely you were here when Peter warned us about it? I went and paid for my licence on the same day Peter told us that the police were checking them.' He chuckled. 'Those three idiots thought they were clever not bothering to get theirs renewed. Now, of course, they'll be forced to pay a fine as well as pay for the road licence.'

Paulo relaxed. If the police were checking road licences, they were sure to have taken a good look at every car parked outside the cafe, including his own. If they had noticed nothing strange about his taxi, then clearly he had nothing to worry about. As far as he could see, his troubles were over – except that never again would he be comfortable in the presence of Peter and Susanna.

Peter entered Janti's just as Paulo was thinking about him and his wife. He seemed much as usual in the check shirt and cotton trousers he wore for work. The only obvious changes in him were the droop of his shoulders and the deepening of lines around his mouth. Instantly he was the centre of a circle of taxi-drivers who all wanted to express their sympathy by offering to bring him tea, coffee or cigarettes.

'We didn't expect to see you here today,' one driver explained.

'Why not? We bury our dead, and life goes on,' Peter said, and straightaway asked for everybody's views on the proposal to form a Ugandan Taxi-Drivers' Union. 'We've talked about it long enough,' he pointed out. 'Now it's time for action.'

Paulo joined in the discussion as eagerly as everybody else, and voted along with the others to request a formal meeting with a trade union official. But he was secretly relieved when an old man came into Janti's and asked Peter, as a special favour, to drive him to Naguru Housing Estate. Guilt, not fear, was Paulo's constant companion whenever Peter was around.

The rest of the day followed the normal Monday pattern. There were profitable runs to be made from the bus station, as well as from outside one of the large mission hospitals. Otherwise, many of the older taxi-drivers regarded Monday as offering their one free evening of the week. Only the younger drivers were prepared to park for hours outside nightclubs where business had slowed down almost to a stop after a busy weekend.

It was Paulo's habit to spend some part of Monday evening with the drivers outside the Bongo Club. He liked to go there to talk with them. If he was hired to take people where they wanted to go, he went. But if nobody wanted the services of his taxi, he didn't really care, and was content to chat and laugh with his colleagues until he decided to go home.

On the Monday after the accident, and after seeing its effect on Peter, Paulo was in no mood to laugh and joke with anybody. Soon after sundown, he was home, facing up to the fact that Charles's death, and the misery of Peter and Susanna, would haunt him for the rest of his life.

There was also the part he had played in the Tank Hill house robbery, and whatever had happened at the house near Mukono. He would have difficulty proving ignorance or innocence with his fingerprints plastered all over the inside of the stationwagon, and the thought scared him.

So far, Paulo had no police record, and therefore his fingerprints had never been taken. But, he asked himself, supposing there came a time when the police were in a position to check his prints against those found on the stationwagon? Stranger things had happened.

He lay on his bed, struggling to find solutions to his problems. He thought about moving to Jinja, Masaka, or even as far away as Kabale in Western Province, to be clear of Peter and Susanna, and the Kampala police. He thought up a dozen schemes for starting a completely new life. Each one seemed to be more impossible than the others.

The only firm idea Paulo produced was the need to get away. In the early hours of the morning he accepted that no matter where he hid in his own country, the police would be able to trace him. He also knew that he would have to go on meeting Peter and Susanna. He saw Peter every day, and Susanna would want him to come to their house. Wearily, he realised that his best plan was to cross the border into Kenya.

Once the decision was made, Paulo spent anxious hours doing sums. He reckoned he could probably go on earning his living as a taxi-driver in Nairobi, so he would have to arrange for the necessary documents to take the car across the border. He also knew that at the current rate of foreign exchange, his Ugandan money would not amount to much in Kenyan shillings. He would need every cent he could collect, to keep him going until he found his way around the Kenyan capital.

It would mean working night and day on the busiest taxi routes during what remained of his time in Kampala, without being able to change the shape of his registration plates. Having the car identified as the one involved in a fatal accident was a risk he would have to take.

But before starting work next morning, Paulo had the wild idea of again visiting the Kisenyi. He wanted to look for somebody who could perhaps fix him up with new number plates and give the vehicle a quick respray in a different colour. He should have known better. The various garage owners and mechanics he approached considered him mad for wanting a full respray completed in a matter of hours.

As for the number plates, they all said the same thing. Besides being difficult to fix on to his model of car, the style of number plate he wanted would, they assured him, look totally out of place.

In the end, Paulo accepted their opinion and stopped trying to persuade any of them to change his registration plates. But he continued to press for a respray.

'What's the hurry?' one mechanic sneered. 'Is this heap of junk hot?'

Paulo indignantly showed the man his log book.

'It most certainly is not stolen, if that's what you mean,' he said. 'Look. You can see for yourself that I'm the legal owner.'

'Well, what's the hurry then?' the mechanic asked again. His eyes narrowed, and it seemed to Paulo that he was looking at the recently repaired headlamp.

'If you must know,' Paulo quickly lied, 'although it's none of your business, I want the car smartened up because there is a chance of selling it.'

This was something the mechanic could understand.

'Bring it here this evening,' he said. 'We'll do a quick job that will make it look respectable, but don't ask for how long!'

They agreed a price for the work, and Paulo drove to the office which issued the documents necessary for taking vehicles outside the country. It took a long time, and he was aware with every passing minute of the money he was losing while he filled in forms and queued at counters.

He finally left the office at noon, and tried to make up for lost time by cruising past the larger hotels, hoping to be hired by guests. He was in luck outside the Speke Hotel. A waiter waved him down and asked him to drive two people to the airport.

His passengers were a foreign couple, and as soon as their bags were placed in the boot of the car, they started arguing in a language which Paulo did not understand. They carried on arguing all the way to Entebbe, and there were moments when he feared they would come to blows.

As they stopped at the military road-block outside the entrance to the airport carpark, his passengers fell silent, and Paulo could see that they looked very nervous. The couple did not relax until his driving licence had been inspected and handed back to him.

A glance in the driving mirror revealed that the man on the back seat had broken out in a heavy sweat, and the woman was nervously biting her lip. Paulo could not wait to off-load these two customers. There was definitely something suspicious about them.

In the carpark, he switched off the engine and turned to receive the fare agreed through the waiter at the Speke Hotel.

'Bring bags. Then we pay,' the man said in English.

Although Paulo objected to being treated like a servant, he was in no position to argue. Also, he wanted to put an end to any dealings with the couple as quickly as possible. There was a strong smell of danger about the pair of them.

So he took their luggage from the boot, and carried it to the entrance of the airport.

'Now, sir, if you will pay me, I'll be on my way,' he said to the man, doing his best to appear courteous and friendly.

The man took some Ugandan currency notes from his pocket and thrust them at Paulo.

'Here. Take this,' he said quickly.

Paulo counted the money. It amounted to less than half the agreed fare.

'This isn't enough,' Paulo said angrily.

The woman burst into a loud gabble of speech which, although he couldn't understand it, left Paulo in no doubt that he was being abused.

The man shrugged and said, 'It is all I have. No more Uganda money.'

'You can pay me in any money you like!' Paulo hotly replied. 'But you've got to pay me.'

'No more Uganda money,' the man repeated. He turned to pick up the bags. He was about to enter the airport to check in his luggage, but Paulo was much quicker to move. He grabbed the bags, and stood,

'No money! No luggage!' he declared.

breathing heavily, daring the man to try taking them from him.

'No money! No luggage!' he declared.

The woman gave a sharp shriek and made as if to hit him with her handbag. Paulo neatly dodged out of her way, but held on to the bags. The scene was attracting interest from people entering and leaving the airport. The woman's companion, husband, or whatever his relationship was to her, had become aware of the interest being taken in the embarrassing scene. He snapped an order at her, and she immediately stopped shouting. He then took out his wallet and offered Paulo ten American dollars.

Paulo urgently wanted to be rid of these people. With a sense of relief, he set down their bags, accepted the money, and turned to walk away. He was stopped by three plain-clothes police officers who made it clear that nobody was going anywhere until a few questions had been answered.

Chapter Six

Paulo and his two passengers were escorted to an office inside the airport. After he had shown his driving licence and identity card, and they their passports, the woman was taken somewhere else to be searched. Paulo and the man were searched on the spot. It was a frightening experience. From the way the search was carried out, Paulo guessed that the police were looking for drugs. He was sick with horror. His other troubles were nothing in comparison to his being suspected of drug smuggling. At least so he thought, until the police took his car keys and went to examine his taxi.

Then his imagination ran wild. He pictured the police spotting the recently repaired headlamp, and realising that his was the car that had been involved in the fatal accident on the Masaka Road. He completely overlooked the fact that very few cars on Uganda's roads were in perfect condition.

Twice he attempted to explain that he had nothing to do with the couple, except as somebody who had driven them to the airport. Each time, he was told to be quiet, that he would soon have a chance to explain what he was doing with the two foreigners.

This did not help at all, and he felt more scared than ever when he was taken to another room and left in the company of a police constable who sat near the door and stared at him.

What seemed to Paulo like hours later, one of the plain-clothes officers arrived to question him, return his car keys, and ask him to make a statement.

There wasn't very much he could say, but the police appeared satisfied with what he had to tell them, and let him know that several airline officials had overheard the row about payment of the taxi fare.

'We're sorry we kept you so long,' the officer said. In spite of his state of shock, Paulo grinned at the idea of receiving an apology from the police. 'I hope you understand that we can't be too careful when dealing with drug traffickers. We were tipped off about these people, and informed that they had an accomplice in Kampala only this morning. We had to check that you were not the accomplice.'

'Did you find anything on them?' Paulo could not resist asking.

The officer looked grim.

'The woman had cocaine as well as heroin hidden in talcum powder containers,' he said. 'There was more in the lining of her suitcase. We suspect that her husband has been foolish enough to swallow plastic packets of the stuff. He doesn't seem to realise how easily it can kill him. He's in the care of a doctor now.'

Paulo was astonished. 'Swallowing plastic packets full of cocaine!' he exclaimed.

The officer laughed at his expression of surprise.

'It's quite common,' he said. 'They can earn enormous amounts of money for carrying drugs from one country to another, so they don't care how they do it. They swallow packets in the hope of passing them normally through their bowels when they reach their destination. Unfortunately, accidents often happen. A packet bursts inside the carrier, and that's the end of him – or her.'

'What were these people doing in Uganda?' Paulo wanted to know.

'Drugs from the Far East used to be smuggled through Kenya to Europe and America. Then the Kenyan authorities found out about the drug smugglers' activities. Now, these smugglers are trying the same thing in our country.'

Paulo eventually left the airport and Entebbe late that night. His mind was full of what he had learned from the police officer, and for the first time in days his own problems took a back seat. He had heard descriptions of the misery brought about by illegal drugs, and the lengths to which people went to make fortunes out of this misery. It sickened him to think that Africans were now taking advantage of this disgusting trade.

Tired and hungry though he was, he drove to the Kisenyi and handed over the car to the mechanic.

'Joseph!' the mechanic called to a youngster who was washing his hands at a standpipe. 'You can't leave yet. That respray job is here.'

Joseph, grumbling, strolled over to look at the car, while the mechanic told Paulo to collect it at about eleven o'clock the next morning.

'Can't you make it earlier?' Paulo protested.

'You're lucky that we can do it at all in such a short time,' the mechanic told him, so Paulo had to be content.

The incident at the airport, coming as it did so quickly after the accident and the robbery with Sulemani and his friends, had left Paulo with an uneasy feeling that somebody, somewhere, was putting a spell on him. Such a run of bad luck was not natural, he told himself. He decided to consult Lucia.

Lucia greeted him in her usual friendly manner, and insisted that he share her supper, as soon as she heard that he had not eaten all day.

As they ate, Paulo mentioned that things had been going wrong for him lately.

'It happens to us all,' Lucia said. 'We all have these ups and downs. Just remember that they never last, and think how dull life would be if we never had a bit of excitement in our lives.'

She already knew about his narrow escape from arrest after agreeing to drive Sulemani's friends. Now, he told her what had happened at the airport. He finished the story with, 'You see what I mean when I say things are going wrong? Everything I touch goes wrong.'

Lucia studied him carefully.

'You must stop thinking that way,' she said. 'You're doing yourself more harm than good. Of course things will go wrong if you expect them to.'

Paulo avoided her eyes and muttered that he thought he might be bewitched.

'Nonsense!' Lucia exclaimed. 'Who would want to bewitch you? Clear your mind of such silly ideas.'

'But if I was bewitched, what could I do about it?' he insisted.

She reached across the table and took his hand.

'I think you're simply tired and unhappy,' she said. 'However, I can see you are worried. Finish your food, and we'll visit somebody I know who will soon tell you whether or not you're bewitched.'

Within thirty minutes they were at the door of a tiny mud and wattle dwelling squeezed between a small mosque and a shop selling ironware.

Lucia knocked, and called, '*Hodi!*'

From within, a weak voice answered, '*Karibu!*'

The door was unlocked, so she and Paulo let themselves in. The single room was lit by a wick floating in a tin of oil, and a thin old man, wearing a *kanzu,* blinked at them from a low bed.

Lucia greeted him fondly, introduced Paulo, and placed a dish of chicken stew on a table beside the bed.

'I've brought your supper, Baba Tembo,' she announced. 'I know how you enjoy chicken stew.'

The old man cackled, propped himself up on one elbow, and started on the stew immediately. While he ate, Lucia talked lightly of happenings in the Kisenyi. She was worried about the lack of water in some areas. She told the old man that a new school was to be opened for homeless children. She laughed about a quarrel between two stallholders in the market.

But as soon as he had finished eating, and had wiped his fingers on the hem of his *kanzu,* she gave the reason for the visit. Baba Tembo peered at Paulo and asked him to describe in detail the incidents which gave him reason to believe he was bewitched.

Paulo took a deep breath and repeated what he had

already told Lucia. Next, Baba Tembo wanted to know about Paulo's eating habits. Did he, the old man asked, prepare his own meals? Did he eat regularly in any particular place? Who else was able to enter his car and room?

When Paulo had answered his questions, Baba Tembo rose creakily from the bed, and tottered to a shelf crowded with pots and jars. He took down a dusty gourd and placed it on the mat where Paulo was seated, telling Paulo to place both hands on the gourd.

Later, Paulo could never be sure whether he really did feel intense heat coming from the gourd, or whether his hands were hot because of nervousness. Whichever it was, he quickly took his hands away.

'I cannot help you until you tell everything,' Baba Tembo said.

'I've told you everything!' Paulo protested.

Baba Tembo's face was without expression. He replaced the gourd on the shelf.

'No,' he said very quietly. 'You have not told me the big trouble.'

'I'm sure he has,' Lucia put in. 'He's told you everything he confided in me.'

'No,' Baba Tembo repeated. 'I cannot help until I know everything.'

Paulo was hot with embarrassment and guilt. Had Lucia not been present, he might have been tempted to tell the old man about the Masaka Road accident. It seemed to him that Baba Tembo could and would help him, although he was not clear in what way. But he could not bring himself to breathe a word about it,

He quickly took his hands away.

with Lucia sitting there. Lucia was a good friend of Peter and Susanna, even though she rarely saw them.

Baba Tembo made it plain that he wished his visitors to leave so that he could sleep.

Lucia turned to Paulo. 'Paulo, is there something else? Something so dreadful that you can't tell me?'

Paulo, unable to speak, miserably shook his head.

'Then, Baba Tembo, you must help him,' she declared. 'This young man is a very good friend of mine. I would trust him with my life. Can't you at least say whether or not he is bewitched, and tell him what to do, if he is?'

Baba Tembo yawned. 'How do I know? He chooses to keep a secret.'

'He doesn't!' Lucia argued. 'Whatever that gourd was supposed to reveal, it must have been wrong! Please, for my sake, give Paulo another chance.'

Wearily the old man once more rose from his bed. This time, he gave Paulo a piece of barkcloth to hold in his right hand. Paulo dropped it hastily as he felt the barkcloth twist like a snake.

'There!' Baba Tembo cried triumphantly. 'The same result! This young man is not telling everything.'

Lucia looked doubtfully at Paulo.

'Come,' she said quietly. 'It's time for us to leave.'

As they opened the door to enter the street, Baba Tembo called after them.

'The only advice I can give your friend, Lucia, is to go far away. And to travel quickly!'

Paulo made up his mind to leave for Kenya as soon as he collected his car next morning.

Chapter Seven

Lucia said very little as she and Paulo walked back to her house. Neither did she invite him in when they reached her door.

He knew that Baba Tembo's words were worrying her. They also worried him. This was why, although he did not say so to Lucia, he had decided to collect the car as soon as possible the next morning. He would then drive across the border into Kenya without saying goodbye to anybody.

He spent most of the rest of the night packing his things, checking that his travel documents were in order, and setting aside the money to be exchanged for Kenyan currency at a *bureau de change*.

Dawn found him sleepless and worn out with anxiety about his future as well as his recent past. He had been chainsmoking, and his mouth tasted like the sole of a street-cleaner's shoe.

He was impatient to pick up the car, but, since it was useless to expect it to be ready so early in the morning, he passed the time first changing his money, and then reading newspapers over several cups of tea in a grubby cafe. It was a dirty place where he was sure not to meet any of his friends. Finally, he walked to the Kisenyi.

Paulo knew that his luck had not changed as soon as he saw his car. It stood in the mechanic's compound, looking like a hideous, overgrown insect. The requested respray must have slipped the mechanic's mind, for the vehicle had obviously been painted by hand, and none too carefully. The roof gleamed vivid red, the bodywork bright yellow, except for a wavy line above the wheels, which was blue.

His mouth fell open, and he stared, horrified, at the mechanic's handiwork.

'What have you done?' he managed to gasp.

The mechanic was immediately on the defensive. 'You insisted on a quick job, and we did our best. Joseph and I think it looks fine.'

'You and Joseph must be off your heads!' Paulo shouted angrily. 'Just look at it. You might at least have done it all one colour. Anyway, you said you would do a respray.'

The argument grew bitter. But Paulo was pressed for time, and he realised that the car in its present condition would take days, if not weeks, to put right. In the end, he paid the mechanic half the agreed price, and drove to his lodgings.

He was in an explosive temper which was not eased by the amount of attention the car attracted on the road. While he collected his bags from his room, after informing his landlady that he was going on safari, a small crowd gathered to gape and wonder at the multi-coloured vehicle in the street outside.

Only when he was clear of the city and heading towards the border was Paulo able to calm down. For one thing, the car's startling appearance caused great amusement at the police road-blocks, so that he was allowed through with the minimum of inspection.

By the time he reached the Ugandan border post, a heavy coating of dust had mercifully reduced the vehicle to a dull brown colour, and nobody seemed to notice anything unusual about it.

During the hour he had to wait to have his papers examined and stamped, Paulo bought a bottle of soda and a bread bun from one of the many street sellers, and sat outside the office with a group of other travellers. Most of them were lorry-drivers returning to Kenya after delivering their loads to various places in Uganda, and Paulo was soon in conversation with them.

When they heard that he was hoping to earn a living as a taxi-driver in Nairobi, they nodded in agreement. All of them said that there was plenty of money to be made from taxis, especially during the tourist season.

But one of them, a man called Samson, warned Paulo that he had better be careful.

'Remember, you'll be a foreigner,' he said. 'If you're caught on any traffic offence, and don't have a work permit, you'll be sent back across the border and not allowed into Kenya again.'

This was news to Paulo. He had assumed that with the correct documents for the car he would be able to do what he liked.

'Oh, don't listen to Samson,' another lorry-driver assured him. 'There are hundreds of Ugandans working in Kenya without permits. My advice to you is just to be careful. Stay out of trouble; and you'll make a small fortune.'

'Where do you plan to stay?' Samson asked. 'I suppose you have plenty of friends in Nairobi.'

Paulo admitted that he only knew the address of one person in Nairobi, and that was a relative of a friend of his. The friend to whom he referred was, of course, Peter, and there was an obvious reason for Paulo not to deliberately seek out any member of Peter's family. So he told the lorry-driver that the man was in big business and probably too important to be approached for lodgings by a mere taxi-driver. He added that he would be glad if anyone could recommend a cheap rooming-house where he could stay.

Samson's name was called from inside the office, and he got up to go and collect his papers.

'Before I leave, I'll give you my address,' he said to Paulo. 'You're welcome to stay with my family until you find a place of your own.'

Paulo was overcome with gratitude. To tell the truth, the nearer he came to crossing into Kenya, the more his mind was filled with doubts and fears as to how he would succeed in starting a new life. Now here was this stranger offering him a temporary home, and, more importantly, the firm hand of friendship.

On the Kenyan side of the border, things moved much more quickly. Paulo was immediately impressed by the neatness of the border post premises, the crisp smartness of the uniformed officials, and the overall efficiency.

He felt in his bones that he was going to like this country, but his happier mood vanished completely when the immigration officer stamping his papers told him that he was only allowed to stay in Kenya for three months. Three months! When Paulo planned to stay a lifetime!

'You can apply to renew the permit,' the officer told him, noticing his dismay, 'but I must warn you that there is no guarantee that your application will be approved.'

Paulo had given Samson's address as his intended residence. He was more grateful than ever to the lorry-driver when he realised that without it he might have had many awkward questions to answer. As things were, he was being treated as a visitor, and not somebody sneaking into Kenya hoping to disappear among the thousands of illegal immigrants.

As soon as his passport and all the forms for the car had been stamped and signed, he got into the car and set off down the road.

Never having been in Kenya before, Paulo drove at a careful pace and often stopped pedestrians to ask directions. It was almost dusk when he parked in Kisumu and ate a meal of *ugali* and fish at a small bar and restaurant.

The proprietor offered him a room, telling him that Nairobi was very far away. He also warned Paulo that it was a difficult journey for a stranger travelling at night. But Paulo was determined to get to the city as soon as possible. He paid for his meal, and set off in the dark.

Many hours later he arrived in the capital city. He was in Nairobi at last, even if he was very tired and nervous. The neon signs distracted his mind from the traffic. They were completely new to him, after Kampala's ill-lit streets. Several accidents were narrowly avoided by the quick-mindedness of Nairobi drivers, who shouted threats and insults at the bewildered Paulo.

He filled up with petrol, using some of his precious Kenyan shillings, and asked the petrol attendant the way to Samson's house. The attendant tried to be helpful, but it was clear that he had never heard of Samson's street, although he knew the district where he lived. He showed Paulo how to get there, and told him to enquire from anyone he saw for the exact directions he needed.

So Paulo once again set off. Never had he dreamed that Nairobi would have sprawled over such a great area. As a taxi-driver, he would have to know every corner, street and alley. He made up his mind to buy a map of the city, and study it well, before he started looking for customers.

It was a relief to find that the petrol attendant's directions were accurate. He was soon in a place called Pumwani, and one of the shopkeepers in a row of kiosks kindly directed him to Samson's house.

To Paulo's surprise, the house was a sturdy stone building in a fenced compound. For some reason, he had expected Samson to be living in one of the rows of municipal housing he had noticed and thought very dirty and depressing, or even in a block of flats.

An elderly man opened the heavy iron gate as soon as Paulo hooted and shouted his name through an opening in the gate. Paulo drove in and parked behind Samson's lorry. Samson was there, smiling broadly, as Paulo stepped from the car.

'I'm glad you made it,' he said. 'Come inside and meet my family. You're just in time for supper. We eat very late here, when I'm at home.'

'Are you sure I'm not disturbing your household?' Paulo peered at the illuminated numerals on his watch. 'It's well after midnight. I'm sorry, but I had to travel fairly slowly, and I had a bit of difficulty finding your house.'

Samson laughed in a friendly way.

'Don't mention it,' he said. 'You did very well, considering this is your first visit to the city. Now come inside. You're very welcome!'

Samson's wife, Miriam, was at the door as Samson led Paulo to the house.

'You are most welcome,' she said, smiling.

Paulo stepped into a comfortably furnished room, blinking in the light from clusters of electric bulbs with gold-coloured lampshades on the walls.

'This is my first son, Benjamin,' Samson said, proudly introducing a teenaged boy who shyly shook Paulo's hand. 'And this is my second son, Elijah.' A boy of about twelve stepped forward. 'And this is my daughter, Rose.'

Two other smaller children were introduced to him, but their names did not register with Paulo. He looked at Rose and took her beautifully formed hand in his. His weary eyes brightened at the glow of her flawless skin, the exquisite slant of her clear eyes, the full, shapely lips, and the long, smooth contours of her throat. He experienced something he had never felt before, something entirely new. His troubles were forgotten. His one thought and desire in life was to have this girl for his own, for ever.

60

Chapter Eight

Paulo, sharing a room with Samson's eldest boy, slept restlessly for what remained of the night. He found it impossible to tear his mind away from Rose. Sitting opposite her at the supper table, he had discovered extra delight in the dimples which appeared in her cheeks each time she smiled. The sound of her soft, low voice was music to his ears.

He was still thinking about her when he took a hasty cup of morning tea with Samson, before going outside to clean his car. Samson joined him as several buckets of water slowly revealed the vehicle's true colours.

'Good heavens, son!' Samson exclaimed, blinking at the sight. 'Whose idea was that?'

Paulo explained how the Kisenyi mechanic had messed things up, and that having a proper respray would have delayed his trip to Kenya.

'And it is a mess,' Samson commented, shaking his head. 'You'll have to do something about it, if you're serious about going into the taxi business.'

He walked around the car. Then he looked at Paulo and waved a finger at him.

'Another thing. Don't try any pirate taxi-ing with those Ugandan registration plates. The police will be on to you as soon as you hit the road. My advice to you is to stay within the law. Apply for a legal work permit. Once you have that, you'll be entitled to register this car in Kenya.'

'I need to start earning money immediately,' Paulo said unhappily. 'I didn't expect to meet with so many difficulties.'

Samson considered the problem for a few moments, glanced at his watch, and said, 'Look, I have to take the lorry down to the warehouse, to pick up the papers for a consignment in Mombasa. On the way, I'll try to see somebody I know who runs a small taxi business. Perhaps he can find a few casual jobs for you, until you clear everything with Immigration.'

Paulo stammered his thanks, but Samson warned that he could not promise anything.

'Go and fill in an application for a work permit this morning,' he advised. 'Rose will take you to the Immigration Department. I'll see you when I get back from Mombasa tomorrow.'

Rose! He was being allowed to spend the morning alone with Rose. Paulo could hardly wait. The car might be a laughable mess on the outside, but, since Rose would soon be travelling in it, he made sure that it was gleamingly spotless inside.

While she ate breakfast with the rest of the family, he showered, shaved, and put on his best shirt and pants. Samson had left a message with his wife regarding the need for Paulo to visit the Immigration Department, and Paulo was pleased to see how quickly Rose responded to the idea of accompanying him.

It took her more than an hour to get ready for the trip to the city centre, and he was in a cold sweat by the time she emerged from the house.

'Oh dear,' her voice was filled with disappointment as she looked at the car. 'Do we have to travel in this? It looks like something out of a circus. Can't we take a taxi?'

'Don't be so fussy!' her mother cried, coming up behind her. 'All you're asked to do is to take this young man to Immigration. Now get in, and show him the way – and see that you come straight home.'

Sulkily, Rose sat in the front seat, next to Paulo. He noticed that she wore a short dress of a floral, silky material, and that her mouth was coated in a thick red lipstick. Her perfume filled the car. He flattered himself that she had taken such great pains with her appearance to impress him, although he secretly believed that she had looked prettier as he had first seen her, without all that stuff plastered on her face.

Her bad mood softened as they drove along. Paulo gathered from what she said that Rose had recently finished training at a secretarial college and was now steadily applying for jobs.

'Sometimes I think I'll never get a job. I've applied for so many,' she complained. 'I'm sick of writing letters and making telephone calls to firms who won't even call me for an interview as soon as they know I've had no previous experience.'

'Don't give up,' Paulo told her, daring to pat her knee encouragingly. 'A smart girl like you is bound to land on her feet.'

'Yes, but how can I be expected to gain experience when nobody will employ me?' she wanted to know. 'And while I'm not earning my own living, I'm forced to live at home and be treated like a child.'

She went on to describe her ambition to have a flat of her own, where she could hold parties, and come and go as she pleased. She complained that she couldn't entertain boyfriends at her father's house.

It seemed to Paulo that Rose held a childish view of the world, and he smiled at the way she assumed that a secretary's salary would allow her to live like a millionaire.

His business at the Immigration Department was brief. A busy clerk gave him some forms to complete, and Paulo decided to play safe by filling in the forms with Samson's help. So he returned to where he had parked the car, and where Rose sat repairing her makeup in the driving mirror.

Wanting to be alone with her for as long as possible, he suggested that they go for a coffee or a soda in one of the nearby cafes. The suggestion delighted her. She knew of a great place, she said. It was a place she visited with her friends whenever she could slip away from home.

The great place turned out to be a beer garden with the smell of roasting meat hanging heavily in the air. It was on the edge of the city, and they had to drive there.

Paulo hid his surprise at the familiar greetings Rose received from the waiters and several men who were drinking beer at the bar. But he was proud to be seen with her. The few other girls around were plain and uninteresting by comparison. Alarm bells rang in his head, however, when Rose demanded beer instead of a soda, and teased him for choosing to drink lemonade.

Two other girls, Maria and Edna, at Rose's invitation, joined their table, and Paulo's anxiety increased as they calmly ordered gin and tonics.

'Make that three gin and tonics,' Rose called to the waiter as he hurried to the bar. 'One beer isn't enough for me.'

'You shouldn't mix your drinks,' Paulo said to her, trying his best to smile. 'In any case, don't you think we should be getting back home?'

Rose responded by taking his hand and placing it against her cheek.

'Oh, Paulo,' she whispered, looking into his eyes so that he felt his bones melting. 'Please let's have a little fun. You've no idea what a miserable time I usually have. My parents are so difficult.'

Paulo would have laid the world at her feet, had it been in his power. The nearness of her knocked every bit of commonsense out of him. He paid for drinks and plates of roasted meat. He even laughed at the silly jokes of Maria and Edna, all because Rose continued to hold his hand, and give him secret smiles full of unspoken promise.

The sun was setting when the party broke up. Maria and Edna went on unsteady legs to sit with a group of young men who had been shouting repeatedly for the girls to join them. Paulo insisted that he and Rose should begin the journey home. In spite of Rose's smiles and kisses, he was shaken by how much the 'little fun' had cost him. Nairobi was proving more expensive than he had expected.

'I must go to the ladies' room,' Rose said, giggling as

'Oh, Paulo,' she whispered, looking into his eyes.

she stumbled and knocked over a chair. 'I'll meet you in the carpark.'

Paulo was excited at the thought of having Rose alone in the car. The problems he had experienced in Uganda were forgotten, as were the gratitude and loyalty he owed to Samson. Nothing mattered except the chance to hold Rose, to express the love which had grown as the day had passed.

He walked through the carpark, found his gaily coloured vehicle in the gathering darkness, leaned against it, and started to light a cigarette. He was too busy thinking about the immediate future with Rose to notice the two stealthy figures creeping up on him. The first blow, from a clenched fist to the head, knocked him to the ground. He lost count of subsequent blows and kicks. But he tried to fight back when greedy hands sought his wallet. It was useless. He was dazed and feeble, and his assailants had run away by the time Paulo staggered to his feet.

Rose arrived while he was fumbling to unlock the door of the car.

'What happened?' she exclaimed, seeing him leaning unsteadily against the car. 'Are you ill?'

Through bruised lips, he explained that he had been mugged, and that his wallet had been stolen.

'Well, it's no good going to the police,' Rose said with a laugh. 'What could they do?'

Paulo had neither mentioned nor thought of going to the police, but he had expected Rose to show some concern and a little sympathy. Miserably, he helped her into the front passenger seat. She needed help because the amount of drink she had taken made her movements awkward. For the first time, he wondered uneasily what effect her obviously drunken state would have on her mother.

There was no way to disguise the fact that she was very drunk. She fell asleep during the drive back to Pumwani, and snored in the most vulgar fashion. Paulo, meanwhile, worried about his lack of money. How was he to manage in a strange country with not a cent to his name? He could not endure the shame of having to ask Samson for a loan, and prayed that Samson could persuade the man with the taxi firm to give him some work.

The more he thought about it the more convinced he became that his run of bad luck was due to his being bewitched, although by whom and why, he did not know.

Suddenly, he wished with all his heart that he had been more frank with Baba Tembo. He was sure that the old man had been in a position to help him. Now it was too late. He drove up to Samson's house with an awful feeling that something terrible was going to happen to him.

Miriam, Samson's wife, came to the front door, looking frightened and worried. Paulo shook Rose's shoulder to awaken her, then helped her from the car.

'Wasser marrer?' she grumbled sleepily, rubbing her eyes. Her mother rushed forward and took her by the arm.

'Leave me alone!' Rose pulled away and stumbled into the house.

Paulo turned to Miriam.

'I'm very sorry,' he said. 'I tried to stop her drinking so much. Please believe that I —'

Miriam quietened him with, 'It's not your fault, young man. It's happened before. Thank God her father is not here. He would have beaten her.'

She drew Paulo into the living room. He protested that he was partly to blame. He realised that he ought to have returned immediately to the house after visiting the Immigration Department.

Miriam sat heavily in an easy chair and wiped tears from her eyes.

'Rose is a wild girl,' she declared. 'She's nearly nineteen years old now, but this drinking and the wild parties have been going on since she was sixteen. Samson and I hardly dare to let her out of our sight.' She gave Paulo a sad smile. 'Samson thinks that the best way to handle it is to give her responsibility, to show her that we trust her. That's why he insisted that she, instead of one of the boys, go with you to Immigration. I could have told him that it was a mistake. I saw how you looked at my daughter, and I knew that she would be able to do what she liked with you.' She gave a sigh.

'Maybe if she could find a job,' Paulo said hopefully.

Miriam gave a sad laugh. 'Job! Who wants to employ a girl who is only interested in a good time? Employers are looking for hardworking people, people interested in a career.'

For the first time she noticed Paulo's bruised and swollen face. She rushed to bathe it with diluted antiseptic while he related how he had received the injuries. She made sympathetic noises in her throat when she heard that his wallet had been stolen.

'There are very nasty people about these days,' she said. 'They don't care who they hurt if there is a chance to steal. But I'm ashamed of my daughter for having taken you to such a place.'

Paulo, who was already finding excuses for Rose's behaviour, telling himself that her bouts of running wild resulted from her parents being too strict, protested that the incident could have happened anywhere. In any case he had been careless. He should have been on the look-out for thieves.

'The fact remains that you lost your money through our daughter taking you to that place,' Miriam said. 'I don't suppose I can make up for all you've lost, but it would make me happier if you would accept something towards it.'

Paulo's pride struggled with his desperate need for money. Finally, he accepted five thousand shillings from Miriam as a loan, to be repaid as soon as he began earning some money.

She left the room and returned with the notes in an envelope.

'I hope you have learned a lesson, and won't carry all your money in your pocket,' she said. Then she added, 'Samson must never know of this. Not about the money. He will understand why I gave that to you. It's about Rose. Please don't ever mention to him that Rose was drunk again. He's a good man, but he has a terrible temper.'

70

Somewhere in the house, a telephone began to ring. Miriam ran to answer it. From different rooms, her sons, Benjamin and Elijah, shouted, 'Is it Dad calling from Mombasa?'

'Keep your voices down, you'll waken the children,' their mother shouted back, before yelling 'Hello? Hello?' very loudly into the receiver.

Miriam was one of those people who cannot trust a telephone to send the spoken word correctly, unless it is bellowed at the top of the voice. Paulo, who was still in the living room, heard every word quite clearly.

'Yes, dear, everyone is all right. Yes, Rose took young Paulo for his immigration papers. Yes, of course they came straight home. You have nothing to worry about. What's that? You want to speak to him? Just a moment. I'll have to call him.'

Paulo ran quickly to the telephone.

'It's Samson,' she whispered, covering the receiver with her hand. 'Remember what I said about Rose. Please don't say anything.'

Samson's voice sounded clear and strong over the telephone wires. He asked Paulo how he had got on at the Immigration Department. Paulo told him quickly what had happened and Samson promised to help him complete the application for a work permit when he returned home from Mombasa the following evening.

'By the way,' he continued, 'I managed to get hold of the man who runs the taxi service I told you about. He wants you to call in and see him at about ten o'clock tomorrow morning. There should be a notepad and pen by the telephone, so you can make a note of the address.'

With trembling fingers, Paulo picked up the pen to scribble the address as Samson dictated it. It was amazing how things changed. One moment he was in the depths of despair, the next he had a new chance to make a success of things. Miriam had given him enough money to get him started, and now her husband was giving him the opportunity to get proper employment and make some money. With a little more good luck, everything would turn out all right.

Later, in bed, he thought lovingly of Rose, who had not appeared at supper. Once he had his work permit, he planned to save as much money as he could, to be in a better position to ask for her hand in marriage. He was confident that under his loving care and attention, and free of the strictness of her parents, she would be content to take care of a home and rear children. He was sure he could quickly stop her wanting to hang around beer gardens with unpleasant companions. When they wanted to go out at night, he would take her to good hotels like the Hilton or the InterContinental or places like that. Nothing but the best would be good enough for his wife.

In spite of his swollen mouth, which had developed a painful split, Paulo could not help grinning to himself as he imagined introducing Rose to his friends, the taxi-drivers in Kampala. They would be so excited by her beauty, that it wouldn't surprise him if a few of them drove straight to Nairobi, hoping for similar luck in finding equally lovely girls.

He fell asleep in the middle of these pleasant imaginings, but they failed to follow into his dreams.

Paulo dreamed that he was back home, driving along the Masaka Road. Something weaving towards him was caught in the headlights, and next he felt a shudder as the car ran over flesh and bones. He heard Peter's voice saying, 'My son is gone, but not forgotten.'

Paulo woke up screaming.

Chapter Nine

Unlike most dreams, Paulo's remained clear in every detail in his mind from the moment he awoke.

Miriam, who believed his frightened screams were the result of the mugging incident at the beer garden, quickly got out of her bed and went to prepare hot milk which she made him drink with a couple of aspirins.

She stayed at his bedside until he had drunk the milk and swallowed the tablets. Then she tucked in the bedclothes, as though he were a small child, and ordered him to sleep. Little did she realise that he was terrified to close his eyes. He was haunted by the memory of the Masaka Road accident.

The fear of being traced by the police was far behind him. It was now something worse than that. He found that it was impossible to be rid of a terrible feeling of guilt. The memory of the accident had faded for a time in the excitement of being in a new country with new friends. But, as he lay in bed, it all came back to him. He could not forget what he had done.

The grieving faces of Peter and Susanna seemed to appear before him in the darkness. He had to bite his swollen lip to stop himself from crying out, 'I'm sorry! I'm sorry!' It was a long time before sleep finally came to him. Even then, he turned and turned all night, sometimes sleeping, sometimes wide awake.

◇

He was neither looking nor feeling his best when, next morning, he set out for his appointment with the owner of the taxi firm. More than anything else, he was disappointed at not catching a glimpse of Rose before leaving Samson's house. He thought about Miriam's comments concerning her daughter. He was convinced that what Miriam called Rose's wildness was due to the way her parents tried to keep her at home all the time. After all, Paulo thought, the girl was nineteen years old. It was only natural that she should object to being treated like a child. It was unfortunate that her way of trying to prove that she was grown up and independent was to drink too much and generally make a fool of herself. He was sure that Rose would soon change, once she realised how seriously he was interested in her.

Paulo did not know what a big mistake he was making. He had had a number of girlfriends in Kampala. He 'played the field' as his taxi-driving bachelor friends referred to their little adventures with women. But underneath, Paulo was a true romantic with a strong belief in real love being able to conquer all. He was still dreaming of a rosy future with Rose, when he arrived at the wooden building behind a petrol station, from where Mr Titus Kamau operated his taxi service.

The girl at the reception desk had just finished answering a telephone call. She wrote something in a large diary, then looked up brightly and asked Paulo if she could help him. He told her of his appointment, and within minutes she was smilingly showing him into an inner office.

Mr Titus Kamau did not respond quite so enthusiastically to Paulo's presence. He gave him a stern look, and grudgingly told him to sit down.

'What happened to your face? Been in a fight?' he wanted to know. 'Samson says you were driving a taxi in Uganda. I should have thought there was good money in that.'

'I was attacked by a couple of thieves. They got away with my wallet,' Paulo explained. 'As for coming to Nairobi, well, I wanted a change. I wanted to see a bit more of the world than Kampala.'

'You should be careful where you go in this city,' Mr Kamau advised, playing with a ruler on his desk. 'They tell me that the crime rate is going up. Anyway, about a job. I can't offer much, especially as, according to Samson, you are in this country on a visitor's permit.'

He glanced out of the window, and his eyes nearly popped as he caught sight of Paulo's car.

'What on earth is that?' he exclaimed in amazement. Paulo indignantly came to the defence of the vehicle which he had owned and looked after carefully for at least two years.

'There's nothing wrong with my car that a good respray won't put right,' he retorted. 'It's perfectly roadworthy, and I drove it from Uganda without any trouble.'

Mr Kamau sat back in his chair and laughed loudly.

'Maybe it is. But you're not driving it for my firm.

What would people say? I can just imagine a client's face if that jazzy heap of junk pulled up to collect him from a nice house.'

'I won't waste any more of your time!' Paulo got to his feet and turned to walk to the door. He had had enough of Mr Titus Kamau. Even though he was more or less penniless, he saw no reason for sitting there, listening to this man insulting his motor car.

'Wait a minute!' Mr Kamau called him back, and Paulo turned, his hand on the door handle. 'Samson is a good man, and I would like to do him a favour. The thing is that it would be tricky, in any case, for you to be driving around with Ugandan licence plates. You see, we work on the basis of drivers using their own vehicles and paying us a commission, a percentage of the fares they charge the customers supplied by us. But if you're interested, maybe you could help Stella here in the office.'

'What sort of help would she want?' Paulo said in an angry voice. He was still annoyed by the way Kamau had treated him, but commonsense and the need to survive made him stop and listen.

Mr Kamau was suddenly friendly.

'Oh, there's plenty to do around here,' he said. 'A fine young man like you could be very useful. You'd be surprised at the amount of business we handle. Besides the taxi business, we own four minibuses which we hire out for carrying wedding guests and that sort of thing. We take children on school outings as well. You could help Stella and perhaps take out one of the minibuses if we're short of a driver.'

It sounded promising. And beggars can't be choosers. Paulo accepted the job, although the salary seemed to him to be pitifully low. Mr Kamau was quick to explain that it was impossible to pay more. Paulo did not have a work permit. So any money he earned would have to be paid from the cash they kept in the office.

'It wouldn't look right in the account books,' he added. 'And remember, I'm sticking my own neck out by giving you a job at all. It's only because you're a friend of Samson's.'

He expected Paulo to begin work at once. There was a store to be cleaned out which he said he was going to use as a drivers' tea-room. At first, Paulo thought it was kind of Kamau to want to help the drivers. According to Kamau, they were usually grateful for a cup of tea after being out on the road for hours. It was Stella who later quietly informed him that Kamau planned to charge for the tea. She said it was just another way Kamau could make a profit.

Paulo took off his jacket and got down to the business of carting out piles of old files, disused batteries, and boxes of rusty spare parts. Then he brushed the place out, and scrubbed the dirty windows. He was sweating by the time he finished, and Stella showed him where he could use the washroom attached to the petrol station.

While he was making himself clean and tidy again, one of the petrol station attendants came into the washroom.

'I see you're working for Kamau,' the man remarked.

'Just helping out for the time being,' Paulo cautiously replied, remembering that he wasn't supposed to be working at all.

'Well, watch him,' the man laughed. 'He's a very clever fellow is our Titus. He'd try to steal your back teeth, if he thought he could get away with it!'

Back in the office with Stella, with the petrol station attendant's comments still ringing in his ears, Paulo learned to answer the telephone, take bookings, and how, with the aid of a map, to contact drivers based nearest to the places from where customers made their calls.

He also watched Stella work out the commission due to Kamau on every trip arranged by the office, and was astonished at the high percentage he charged. He wondered why these drivers didn't go it alone, and keep all their earnings to themselves.

Mr Kamau left for lunch in the city, and did not return. During his absence, Paulo grew to admire Stella's efficiency. She seemed to carry a map of Nairobi in her head, and connected taxis with customers without a moment's hesitation. Although she was nowhere near as attractive as Rose, he liked her pleasant little face and trim figure. He also liked the way she accepted him as a working colleague, and did her best to show him the ropes. She told Paulo that she had been Mr Kamau's assistant since leaving school four years ago.

'Someone else takes over from me in the evening,' she said. 'You'll meet him before you and I leave. His name is Mungai. Don't be put off by his manner. I think that working alone at night is the reason why he always sounds as if he's looking for a fight.'

At about four in the afternoon, Stella made tea and shared a small bunch of bananas with Paulo. They were in the middle of this afternoon meal when several taxi-drivers came into the office to arrange to fill up with petrol. Only then did Paulo realise that Kamau owned the petrol station too. Stella signed a form authorising the supply of petrol. When the men had gone, Paulo asked why they had not filled their tanks in the city.

'It's one of Mr Kamau's rules,' Stella said. 'All our drivers have to buy their petrol from him. It's all right. He lets them have it on credit.'

'And probably lets them have it at a discount price?' Paulo suggested.

Stella looked embarrassed for a moment.

'Well, no,' she murmured, 'he has to charge them a little interest on their monthly petrol accounts. He says that he's letting them use his money for a month, so he has to get some of it back this way.'

Paulo nodded grimly. The more he heard about Mr Titus Kamau, the less he liked the idea of working for him. He had no reason to change his opinion after Stella revealed that Kamau headed a finance and insurance company which arranged loans for people who wanted to buy cars. Very often they were desperate to find a way to make some money and saw the taxi business as a means of doing that. Titus Kamau used a complicated hire-purchase system, with conditions all in his favour. Nearly all the drivers were well and truly in his grip and were handing over most of their earnings to him.

'Surely it's illegal?' Paulo exclaimed. 'It sounds like slave labour to me!'

Stella glanced nervously around, to see if they were being overheard.

'No,' she said. 'Mr Kamau is really helping the drivers. The loans he gives them cover the full cost of the vehicles, so they don't have to find the deposit. And he has a special arrangement with six Nairobi hotels for our taxis to be based at their entrances. So they get customers from among the hotel guests as well as receiving calls from this office. They always have plenty of business.'

Paulo shrugged his shoulders. In his view, a good driver with a well-maintained car ought to be able to manage very well on his own, without the help of Mr Titus Kamau.

Mungai arrived shortly after six in the evening. Stella had not exaggerated when she described his unpleasant nature. He was a short, slight, middle-aged man, and his eyes narrowed when Stella introduced Paulo to him.

'Let's hope you'll be able to relieve me,' he said in a high voice. 'It's months since I've had a night off. But I suppose you're only interested in a job which leaves your evenings free.'

Stella quietly signalled to Paulo to ignore Mungai's bad manners, and looked relieved when somebody came in with a canvas bag containing the day's takings from the business at the petrol station.

She began checking the money against the receipts, while Mungai answered a stream of telephone calls.

Paulo anxiously wondered when he would be allowed to go back to Samson's house so he could see his beautiful Rose. Besides, he was getting very hungry for a decent meal. It seemed a long time since his breakfast of mealie porridge and tea. The tea and bananas which Stella had given him had, if anything, increased his appetite.

'Won't be long now,' Stella said, giving him a sympathetic smile, and finishing some rapid additions on a calculator. 'Then, if you'll help me to carry this bag through to the safe, we can be on our way.'

Although she worked quickly, it was after seven before the receipts were checked, the amounts entered into a cashbook, and filed. Paulo, thankful to be on the point of leaving, picked up the canvas bag and almost ran with it into Kamau's office

There Stella unlocked a steel safe hidden behind a filing cabinet. The top shelf of the safe already held stacks of banknotes and bags of coins. Below it sat neat piles of clear plastic folders containing documents concerning the luckless taxi-drivers who had more or less sold themselves to Titus Kamau.

'Mr Kamau will take everything to the bank tomorrow,' Stella explained, noticing Paulo's surprise at the amount of cash kept in a place with such poor security. 'Somebody from his finance company usually collects the money for banking every morning, but for the last couple of days the man has been off sick.'

Paulo was about to remark that the petrol station was obviously doing good business, when there was a sudden loud noise in the outer office. Mungai shouted

He, Stella and Mungai lay bound and gagged.

something which sounded alarmingly like a warning. Then there was a strangled cry, and a heavy thud as something fell to the floor.

Instinctively, Paulo leapt forward to slam the door of Kamau's office. Before he was halfway there, a man with a stocking covering his face, and waving a heavy *panga*, rushed in with such speed that Paulo was flung against the desk. Stella cowered, terrified, against the open safe. The intruder dragged her roughly aside.

Paulo, acting more from outrage than bravery, jumped on the bully's back. He might have succeeded in wrestling the man to the ground, but two other men entered the office at that moment. Stella screamed as Paulo was punched and kicked until he lost consciousness. When next he opened his eyes, he, Stella and Mungai lay bound and gagged in the small space behind Kamau's desk. From the outer office came the urgent ringing of the telephone.

Chapter Ten

As his mind cleared, Paulo noted with alarm that although Stella struggled to free herself, Mungai was lying very still and looking strangely grey. Paulo managed to edge closer to Mungai, and was trying to see if he was breathing, when a nightwatchman and several strangers rushed into the office.

Everyone talked at once and clumsy attempts at first aid were made.

The nightwatchman was mainly interested in telling how he had spotted the thieves leaving with a heavy bag, and seen them jump into another vehicle when their own refused to start.

'I knew rightaway that something was wrong!' he said over and over again.

It was only after Stella was untied and the gag removed that anybody thought to contact the police, and it was Stella's own trembling fingers that finally dialled 999.

'Better ask for an ambulance, too,' Paulo quietly advised, as soon as she was through to the emergency service. 'Mr Mungai is in a bad way.'

Even when the ropes binding his wrists and ankles, and the soiled rag which had been stuffed into his mouth, had been removed, Mungai still remained flat on his back, his glazed eyes staring at the ceiling, and his breath rattling in his throat.

Stella, except for a badly bruised shoulder where she had been pushed roughly away from the open safe, seemed to have come through the ordeal with little damage, apart from shock. In no time, she was busy trying to contact Kamau at his home. Paulo, on the other hand, had taken a thorough beating, and his whole body was a mass of pain. All he wanted to do was to crawl into bed and sleep for a week. But the arrival of the police and an ambulance for Mungai made it necessary for him to stay where he was to answer questions.

There was a tricky moment when he was asked how he came to be in Kamau's office. Paulo hesitated over his reply. Stella, who knew that he could not tell the police that he was working there, quickly came to the rescue.

'He's a friend of mine,' she said. 'We were planning to have a meal together, after I finished work.'

Even so, a worse blow than any he had received from the robbers hit Paulo when he realised that the car in which the thieves had escaped was his own. There could be no doubt. The nightwatchman, thrilled at being the centre of attention, quickly described his astonishment at the sight of such a gaily coloured vehicle parked near Mr Kamau's office at the time he came on duty.

'It was the only one parked out there!' he said proudly, pleased to show off his good memory. 'And that's the one they took. They must have had the keys, because they were in it and off in a matter of seconds.'

Paulo immediately felt in his pocket for his car keys.

They were gone. Obviously, they had been taken or had fallen out of his pocket while he was being roughed up.

Now the policemen were looking at him suspiciously. At least a couple of them were. The third was transmitting details of the car so that patrols could keep a look-out for it. It came as no surprise to Paulo that he should be asked to accompany the police to the station.

'I'll join you as soon as I can,' Stella told him as he got into a police car. 'I can't leave the office until I've spoken to Mr Kamau.'

A feeling of helplessness came over him when he was being questioned at the police station. Why, the sergeant questioning him wanted to know, was he in the inner office with the wide-open safe, if, as he claimed, he was only on Kamau's premises to meet his girlfriend? And, the sergeant added, wasn't it a strange coincidence that the thieves should have the keys to Paulo's car in case anything went wrong with their own?

No matter how Paulo argued that he had nothing to do with the robbery, and pointed out that he had been assaulted as well as bound and gagged along with Stella and Mungai, his protests fell on deaf ears. The policemen concerned were not the most brilliant or educated members of the force, and their main interest lay in claiming credit for an arrest. The fact that Paulo was a Ugandan was regarded by them as a strong indication that he was in their country to commit a crime.

Samson and Stella arrived at the police station within minutes of each other. Samson, having returned from

Mombasa, and sharing his wife's anxiety about Paulo's failure to come back to the house, had gone looking for him. The nightwatchman at the petrol station had been only too eager to relate the night's events, and Samson had hurried to find out why his young friend was in police custody.

Stella was there to reaffirm her story that Paulo was simply a friend who happened accidentally to be on the premises when the thieves raided the place. The two of them wasted a whole hour trying to explain that Paulo was innocent.

Then a call came through from another police station to say that the car left behind by the thieves had earlier been reported as stolen by the true owner. Paulo's car had been found abandoned in another part of the city.

'You see!' Samson declared as soon as he was given the information. 'If my friend Paulo was working with the thieves, surely they would not have dumped his car along some roadside?'

'Ah!' replied a constable, grinning wisely. 'How do we know that that's not where he was supposed to pick it up?'

The silliness ended when an officer came from another part of the building, and curtly ordered his subordinates to explain what all the fuss was about. By this time, Paulo had been thrown into a cell-like room which reeked of urine and vomit. He was brought out to tell his side of the story, and was past feeling any relief at hearing the officer declare that he was to be released immediately. Wearily, he thanked Stella for her support, then dragged himself into Samson's car.

He was in no condition to respond to Samson's enthusiastic praise of Stella as a girl of strong character, a girl of whom any man could be proud. He did, however, move uneasily when Samson complained about Rose.

'If only my daughter was like that young woman who flew to defend you! Oh, Paulo, Rose is our sorrow – Miriam's and mine. We've tried to do our best for her, but somehow we have failed to turn her into the sort of person we wanted her to be. That girl is a constant source of worry to us.'

Miriam came running to the car the moment she heard it turn in at the gate.

'Thank God!' she exclaimed, seeing Paulo beside her husband. Then, as she took a closer look at him, 'Good heavens, son, what has happened to you?'

Between them, she and Samson assisted Paulo up the veranda steps. The beating he had taken from the robbers made his body ache worse than ever now. His arms and legs hurt at the slightest movement, and his groin and stomach were suddenly giving him agony. Afterwards, he was never very sure how he came to be in bed, although at some stage he was aware of somebody, presumably a doctor, giving him an injection.

For the following two days he drifted through a series of nightmares in which Peter, Susanna, their son Charles, and the raid on Kamau's office were all muddled together. On the evening of the second day he awoke to find Miriam at his bedside. Her kindly face broke into a beaming smile as he recognised her.

'You're better!' she proclaimed. 'I knew my prayers would be answered! Let me call Samson. He's been so worried about you.'

Samson entered the bedroom and took Paulo's feeble hands in his.

'How are you feeling, my boy?' he asked. 'Dr Macharia wanted us to take you to hospital, but my wife insisted that you would be better off in her care.'

'I feel … Well, I think I feel a lot better,' Paulo whispered, noticing that he was free of pain. 'I'm just a bit weak. That's all.'

'I'm glad,' Samson nodded approvingly. 'And there's more good news. It now turns out that the robbery was organised by a clerk in Kamau's city office, somebody in his finance and insurance company, the person who collected money to be banked every day. According to what Kamau has just told me over the phone, the man pretended to be off sick, so that there would be at least a couple of days' takings in the safe.'

'How did they know he was the one?' Paulo asked.

Samson smiled. 'One of the more intelligent policemen made a few enquiries among the neighbours about the man's state of health,' he replied. 'For a very sick man, the clerk spent an awful lot of time in the local bar!'

'How is Rose?' Paulo put the question carefully. It was an indication of his recovery that his thoughts should quickly turn to the object of his love.

'That girl will be the death of me,' Samson said sadly. 'She's decided that she wants to be a hairdresser. Besides paying for her education and two years' secretarial course, now she's asking me to pay for a hairdressing course.'

'Are you talking about me?' Rose asked as she bounced into the room, and immediately Paulo flushed with joy at seeing her. She wore a *suka* which set off the graceful lines of her shoulders and arms, and her face was clear of makeup.

'I'm glad to see you're better!' she said laughingly to Paulo. 'Mother will now be able to spend more time on the rest of us. She has been at your bedside night and day.'

'I don't regret it,' Miriam said from the doorway. 'And here is somebody else who was willing to sit and pray with me, as well as help make the patient comfortable.'

Behind her Paulo saw Stella's eager face.

'Paulo!' Stella cried. 'How wonderful to see you back in the land of the living. Miriam and I have certainly proved the power of prayer.'

'With a little help from the doctor!' Miriam put in.

'Anyway,' Stella continued, coming forward and sitting on Paulo's bed, 'I'm very glad that you are recovering – which is more than can be said for poor Mungai. I've just been to the hospital. The poor man has a fractured skull. The doctors will only say that his condition is fair.'

Before Paulo could say a word of sympathy for the luckless Mungai, Rose went out, slamming the door.

'Pay no attention,' Miriam said, glancing nervously at her husband. 'Our daughter can be very bad-mannered.'

Stella's embarrassment was evident.

'Did I say something to upset her?' she asked.

'No, child,' Samson looked grim. 'Rose will have to learn one day that she can't always be the centre of attention.'

Paulo desperately wanted to explain that it was Rose's company that he wanted, and he hardly listened as Stella told him that his car, after being dusted for fingerprints, was now awaiting collection at police headquarters. When she eventually accepted an invitation to supper, and joined Samson and the rest of his family at table, Miriam brought a tray of food to Paulo. She lingered in the room while he did his best to please her by trying to choke down a few mouthfuls, but he sensed she had more on her mind than making sure that he ate his meal. Suddenly she sat down on the side of the bed and looked at Paulo.

'Tell me, Paulo,' she said, 'what really brought you to Nairobi? I ask because some of the things you shouted while you were delirious made me wonder.'

Paulo's mouth went dry. He could no longer pretend to show the slightest appetite.

'What sort of things?' he muttered, avoiding Miriam's eyes.

She sat on the bed, and took his hand.

'Well, most of all you kept begging someone called Peter to forgive you,' she said. 'Once you screamed the name Charles, and said something about blood on the road.'

'Did anybody else hear me?' Paulo shuddered as he spoke.

Miriam patted his hand.

'No, son. Only me. But if you're in trouble, you must know by now that Samson and I will do all we can to help you.'

Tears stung Paulo's eyes. He was physically weak, and tired of trying to keep his guilty secret which he realised could very well destroy the remainder of his life. He also saw that his recent troubles all sprang from his desire to avoid the consequences of the accident on the Masaka Road. Breaking down completely, he allowed the tears to flow as he stammered out the story to Miriam. When the last unhappy words trailed away, she hugged him.

'From what you have told me,' she said quietly, 'the accident was unavoidable, and your friends, Peter and his wife, seem to be good people. You were wrong, Paulo, to behave this way.'

'I'll never be able to face them again,' Paulo said miserably, shaking his head.

'So what will you do?' Miriam put the question sadly. 'It's clear to me that running away from the problem has brought you nothing but trouble. You can expect disaster after disaster to strike you, unless you are prepared to go home and be honest with Peter and his family. For your own peace of mind, Paulo, you will have to speak out.'

He knew that she was right, and he didn't object when she suggested calling Samson to give his opinion.

Samson heard the story from Paulo.

'You've been very foolish, my boy,' he said. 'If you had reported the accident immediately after it happened, even if you didn't stop to attend to the victim, you would soon have been in the clear. Now, of course, if your friend Peter decides to take you to the police, you'll end up in court with a lot of explaining to do.'

'Are you brave enough to face all that?' Miriam asked Paulo.

He nodded slowly.

'I'll try hard to be,' he replied.

In the next few days, Paulo prepared to return home to Uganda. Now that his mind was made up, he deliberately avoided thinking about how he would approach Peter, or what might be the outcome of their reunion when he reached Kampala.

Samson and Miriam gave him every help and encouragement they could, telling him over and over again that he was welcome to come back and stay with them whenever he wished. And Paulo planned to return. Since he had left his bed and stopped being an invalid, Rose's attitude towards him grew warmer with every passing day. She playfully stroked his hair in passing, as he sat reading a newspaper on the veranda, and, as soon as his car was collected from the police headquarters, asked to be taken for a ride.

Although he desperately wanted to, Paulo refused to take her anywhere, because he had no wish to upset Miriam with another drunken performance. He was also amused to notice flashes of jealousy from Rose whenever Stella called to see him, which led him to believe his feelings for her were returned with the same intensity.

On the night before his departure, Miriam made a

farewell supper which was really a feast, and Stella was invited. She arrived at the house carrying a parcel.

'A little farewell present which I hope will be useful,' she explained, as Paulo opened the parcel and brought out two smart cotton shirts.

'It's very kind of you, Stella,' he said. 'You've been a good friend to me.'

Everybody except Rose admired the shirts, and as they gathered around the table, she took no part in the conversation. Several times Paulo addressed remarks to her, but she ignored him, and despite the bright chatter and jokes from everybody else, the meal was spoilt for him. He had wanted this particular evening to be memorable, and he had intended at some stage to ask Rose to wait for him and marry him when he returned to Nairobi. There was no chance of that, however, for after supper Rose went off to her room, and Samson asked Paulo to accompany him when he drove Stella home. Before entering her house, Stella pushed a slip of paper into Paulo's hand.

'This is my address,' she said. 'Write to me if ever you think I can help you – and have a safe journey home.'

She stood on her tiptoes and gave Paulo a kiss on the lips. Then she turned and ran to the door of the house.

'That's a wonderful girl,' Samson remarked as they headed back to his house. 'If you have any sense, Paulo, my boy, you'll finish your business in Kampala, and come back and marry her.'

Paulo could not stop himself saying, 'I'd rather marry Rose!'

'What!'

Samson pulled in at the roadside, and switched off the car's engine. He turned to face Paulo.

'You must be mad,' he said. 'Rose is my daughter, and I tell you seriously that I wouldn't wish her on my worst enemy. The girl is lazy, selfish, deceitful, and any man who marries her will be miserable before he's two steps away from the church.'

'I can't help it,' Paulo replied. 'Rose is the only one for me. I think – and please, Samson, don't be offended – I think that perhaps you and Miriam are too strict with her. You both seem to forget that she's nineteen years old. She's a woman, and no longer a child. She does wild things only because she wants to show her independence.'

Samson sighed.

'You wouldn't say such things if you knew how we have tried to show that girl love and trust, to build her confidence. In return, all we've got is shame and unhappiness. In the short time we've known you, Miriam and I would love to have you as a son-in-law, but we are both too fond of you to burden you with Rose.'

Stubbornly, Paulo insisted that he would risk anything to marry her, and asked Samson's permission to speak to her before he left for Uganda. Samson switched on the engine.

'Very well,' he said. 'Ask her to marry you if you must. I advise you, though, not to place much trust in her answer, if she says yes.'

They drove in silence for the rest of the way home, and were startled to see Miriam, a damp handkerchief to her streaming eyes, standing at the open gate.

'It's Rose!' she sobbed, before either of them had a chance to ask what was wrong. 'She's run away! Everything has gone from her room, and the nightwatchman says a car was waiting at the end of the road for her.'

Paulo felt as if the ground was giving way beneath his feet, but Samson looked at him and said, 'Consider yourself lucky. You have been saved from a lifetime of trouble.'

Chapter Eleven

Paulo completed the return journey to Kampala hardly remembering any of the towns through which he passed, or even crossing the border. He was in a state of shock.

He had left behind a sad, bewildered household. Miriam had completely gone to pieces over the disappearance of her daughter, and lay weeping in a darkened bedroom. Samson, for the sake of the younger children, had hidden his misery under a cloak of anger, but Paulo saw how grief had drawn deep lines on his face.

Their parting had been brief. They both wanted to avoid talking about what Rose had done. Samson had brushed aside Paulo's promises to repay the money borrowed from Miriam as quickly as he could.

Once on his home ground, Paulo drove to his old lodgings where his landlady was pleased to see him and gladly handed him the key to the room he had previously occupied. He was too tired and depressed to do more than wash and lie down on the bare mattress of the bed. What he needed to say to Peter and Susanna took a poor second place in his mind. He could think of nothing other than Rose packing her bags and sneaking away. Where had she gone? And with whom? He went over every gesture she had made and every word she had spoken which had caused him to believe that he meant something special to her.

He tried desperately to find excuses for her behaviour. He even tried to convince himself that her disappearance meant that she could not bear to be separated from him, that she was even at that moment in Kampala, searching for him.

An urgent knocking at the door of his room brought him back to reality. He got up and scrambled into his trousers.

'All right! Just a minute! I'm coming!' he shouted.

As soon as he unlocked the door, his landlady burst in.

'Paulo,' she screamed, 'you must drive me to Peter and Susanna's house! There's a boy here who says it's on fire!'

The landlady, a cousin of Susanna's, moaned and sobbed hysterically as Paulo drove as fast as he could to Natete.

The glow of the fire could be seen from Masaka Road, and when they reached Peter's compound, the place was alive with people throwing water on the flames.

The appearance of a fire engine received a mixed welcome. Many loudly shouted that it was too late to be of any use. Paulo overheard people saying that an oil lamp was responsible for starting the fire. Somebody else argued that it was more likely to have been a pressure stove which had caused the blaze.

Whatever the cause, the house was alight from top to bottom. Dense smoke poured out from somewhere at the back, and yellow tongues of flame leapt from the front windows.

The firemen's water hoses were having little effect. Suddenly, a fireman staggered from the building, carrying Peter, limp and lifeless, across his shoulders. Paulo ran forward and helped the fireman to place the unconscious man on a stretcher which was immediately lifted into a waiting ambulance. The ambulance, its siren screaming a warning, was on its way to hospital even as the back doors were still being closed.

'Is there anybody else in the house?' Paulo asked a fireman who was rushing to check the water pressure.

'I hope not. The roof's about to cave in!' the fireman shouted over his shoulder.

'My mother! My mother's still inside!' somebody nearby cried, and Paulo turned quickly to find Peter's son, James, weeping bitterly.

'Susanna!' Paulo yelled, forcing a path through the crowd of helpers and onlookers, and running into the blazing house.

The intense heat made his clothes, which were drenched from splashed water, steam. It almost forced him back, but with a handkerchief pressed to his face he battled blindly on. The smoke, which he was sucking into his lungs, made each step more painful than the last.

For most of the time he was only aware of the urgent need to find Susanna. Then, as if from nowhere, the fireman to whom he had spoken earlier appeared alongside him. Because Paulo was familiar with the old house and its many rooms, he was able to grope his way along to the bedrooms.

He forced himself to ignore the blazing ceiling showering sparks on to his head, as well as the terrible heat creeping steadily towards him from where part of the roof had already collapsed. Instinct led him to one door. The hot metal of the doorknob made him gasp with pain, and the door itself was either locked or distorted by heat, for it refused to budge, even when Paulo threw himself against it.

The fireman had to use his hatchet to smash the whole door before it fell open, and the two men, coughing and spluttering, stumbled into the room. Susanna lay in a heap near the bed. They were only able to make out her silhouette through the thick cloud of smoke.

Together they dragged her into the passage, and beat out the flames which sprang like magic from the folds of her *busuti*. The fire was now gaining on them, and the smoke was thickening.

Both Paulo and the fireman were fighting to breathe and they were making slow progress with Susanna's limp body hanging between them. Suddenly other figures emerged from the smoke. Firm hands grasped Paulo, the fireman and Susanna, and somehow hauled the three of them to safety seconds before what was left of the roof crashed down.

◇

Paulo lay in hospital for several weeks. He was treated for serious burns on his head, shoulders and hands. He was heavily sedated for most of the time, and lived in a

They were making slow progress with Susanna's limp body hanging between them.

world of dreams and nightmares filled with bouts of the most terrible pain.

One day after the medical staff had reduced the amount of drugs he was to have, and allowed visitors to see him, Paulo opened his eyes to find Peter standing at the foot of his bed. Without greeting the old man, Paulo mumbled through his bandages.

'Susanna … What happened to Susanna?'

'She's all right – thanks to you,' Peter replied. 'You saved her life. The firemen would never have found her without you to lead the way. We both owe you more than we can ever repay, Paulo.'

Paulo made a slight movement, as if trying to shake his head.

'No,' he whispered. 'You don't understand. When I tell you, you'll hate me for the rest of your life. I killed Charles.'

He had made the confession bluntly, because he was too sick to search for words, and he no longer cared what became of him. The injuries he had received in the fire had convinced him that he could suffer nothing worse. Peter sat heavily on a chair by the bed, and placed his hand very, very gently on Paulo's shoulder.

'Are you telling me that you were the driver involved in Charles's death?' he asked. 'Are you saying that you knocked somebody down and didn't bother to stop to see how badly hurt they were, Paulo? I would never have believed it if I hadn't heard it from your own lips.'

Paulo moved a hand as if to interrupt, but Peter went on as if he had not seen anything.

'You are young, and I can well imagine how you felt at the time, as well as afterwards. And I can also believe you would have acted differently, had you known the person you hit was Charles.

'But what I have tried so hard to impress upon all you taxi-drivers is that you must do your best for any accident victim, regardless of whether or not he is known to you. Charles was drunk. I know that. The doctors at the hospital told us that he was so full of liquor they were surprised he was able to walk. The fact that he was killed on the road was probably more his own fault than anybody else's. I suppose he practically rolled under your car? Well, it's over. We must put it behind us and carry on as usual.'

'How can I?' Paulo's muffled exclamation sounded bitter. 'How can I carry on as usual? Every time you see me, you'll be reminded that I had a part in your son's death. As for Susanna, what will she think of me?'

Peter stared out of a nearby window.

'You wonder what she'll think of you?' he said. 'Imagine how I feel when I tell you that I caused the fire which almost cost both our lives.'

Paulo thought he hadn't heard him correctly.

'What do you mean? You didn't burn your own house down.'

'It's true, I did,' Peter said. 'That night, after Susanna had gone to arrange things for the morning breakfast, before getting ready for bed, and our boys had gone off with some friends, I fell asleep in a chair in the living room. I'd had a glass or two of whisky, so I slept heavily. I woke up to find myself in a room on fire. I know how it happened. I'd left a lighted cigarette balanced on a saucer. It must have rolled off, on to a straw mat. Anyway, mat, curtains and some cushions were all burning.

'By the time I brought water from outside to put out the flames, the fire had got a strong hold on everything in the room. I was foolish enough to try fighting it on my own.' He smiled grimly. 'Can you believe that I didn't want Susanna to see what a wreck I had made of her living room? I made matters worse by leaving the door open every time I ran to the water tank. A stiff breeze did the rest. I would never have believed that a fire could spread so fast.'

'Surely Susanna must have smelled smoke?' Paulo suggested.

'Oh, she did,' Peter agreed. 'And it was Susanna who sent our gardener to call the neighbours. Our big mistake was to spend too long thinking we could control the fire. We forgot that an old house such as ours is a mass of dry timber. Then when things became really bad, Susanna refused to leave without her treasures, as she calls them. She wanted to take the family albums, her Bible and her rings and things. She locked me out of the bedroom, where she kept her precious things, because I threatened to carry her out of the house if necessary. I set off to bring somebody to break down the door and help me drag her out. That's when a beam fell and trapped me in a corner. I couldn't move, and I was suffocating from all the smoke when those firemen came along and pulled me free.'

'Peter, don't blame yourself. It was an accident! It

could have happened to anybody.' Paulo could not bear the distress in Peter's voice.

'Yes, but it was an accident which nearly cost me my wife,' Peter whispered, almost to himself. Then, looking straight at Paulo, he added, 'Susanna must never know the truth about the road accident involving Charles. Apart from the fact that you've always been her favourite among the young drivers, she can do without any more shocks. The doctors say she must have complete rest for at least a month, so I'm taking her home to the village, where she'll stay until I rebuild the house at Natete.'

Their conversation was interrupted by an uproar in the corridor outside the ward. The other patients and their visitors turned expectantly as the doors swung wide to admit six grinning taxi-drivers followed by an angry little nursing sister. The sister was insisting that Paulo could not see more than one visitor at a time, but the drivers marched straight to Paulo's bedside, and the sister retired, threatening to have them thrown out.

'Hi, taxi-man! How's the hero?' Musa called cheerfully. 'Getting inside this place to see you is harder than getting into State House.'

'This is the fourth time we've been here,' Musoke announced after greeting Peter.

The other four drivers stood happy but uncertain what to do in these unfamiliar surroundings.

'Where've you been hiding, man?' Musa went on. 'Until the night of the fire, we all thought you had married a rich widow and flown to America.'

'I had a short holiday in Kenya,' Paulo told him,

glad that the bandages hid the expression on his face. 'Now tell me how things are with you.'

'No, you're what we are here for,' another driver laughed. 'In case you haven't had a chance to read the newspapers, we cut out the bits mentioning you, and brought them with us.'

He placed a grubby envelope on the bed.

'Remove that immediately!' snapped a passing nurse. 'The dressings on that patient are supposed to be kept completely free of germs.'

Musa hastily put the envelope on Paulo's locker and said, loudly enough for everybody in the ward to hear, 'Yes, my friend, you're really famous.'

Paulo flushed with embarrassment as one of the drivers opened the envelope and read each newspaper cutting aloud.

'So you're the Natete fire hero, are you?' the man in the bed opposite Paulo's called across the ward. 'We're very proud to meet you. We've been wondering how you came to be in such a mess. These nurses will never tell anybody anything, except to tell us to mind our own business.'

The newspaper reporters had written a number of descriptions of the fire and Paulo's part in the rescue. But Paulo considered they had gone too far with one headline which read, '*Gallant Young Taxi-Driver Defies Death*'.

While he was pleased to see his friends again, he was relieved when an elderly doctor came into the ward and ordered every one of them out. The drivers did not argue with him, as they had done with the nursing

'Yes, my friend, you're really famous.'

sister. They went quietly away, only pausing to wink and give Paulo the thumbs-up sign. Peter stayed to put the fruit and cigarettes he had brought in Paulo's locker.

'Get well soon, son,' he said. 'And don't worry any more about anything.'

'I'll try,' Paulo promised. 'At the moment, my head is not very clear.'

'I want to see you on the road again – we all do,' Peter told him. 'And to give you something to look forward to, I took your car and had it resprayed. It's now a very nice pale cream colour. Whatever possessed you to get it painted like an icecream barrow?'

Paulo laughed for the first time in weeks.

'Oh, that's a long story. I'm very grateful, Peter. Many thanks. I can't wait to see the car. As soon as the bandages come off, I'll be behind the wheel.'

'You'd better be,' Peter smiled.

For a moment, the two men looked at each other with deep affection, before Peter raised his hand in a little salute and said, 'Take care of yourself, Taxi.'

Paulo tried to be cheerful, but he found that his voice sounded strange and there were tears in his eyes.

'You, too, Taxi – and thanks!'

Glossary

busuti (page 102) traditional dress for women. Also called *kigomezi* or *kigayaza*

kanzu (page 50) long white robe worn by men

kikoyi (page 17) piece of cloth worn as a wrap, or sarong-type garment called *suka*

matoke (page 33) green plantain, staple food in parts of Uganda

murram (page 2) red clay

shamba (page 18) garden

suka (page 7) a piece of cloth tied under the arms as a dress

waragi (page 19) local alcohol distilled from bananas

Discussion

1 Do you think Paulo got off too easily? What should be the punishment for the crime he committed? Which was worse – knocking the man down or failing to stop?

2 Many young men in Africa today are tempted to commit crimes in order to make money to live. What can governments do to help prevent this happening?

3 Paulo meets two good men – Peter and Samson. Could you forgive Paulo for killing a relative of yours and not trying to help him? Would you try to stop someone marrying your daughter if you knew she was like Rose?

4 Everything is changing very rapidly in Africa today, even relationships between parents and children. How do you think the problems between Rose and her parents could have been solved?